2 KINGS

The Fall of Israel and Judah

John MacArthur

THOMAS NELSON
Since 1798

MacArthur Bible Studies

2 Kings: The Fall of Israel and Judah

© 2016 by John MacArthur

Published in Nashville, Tennessee, by Nelson Books, an imprint of Thomas Nelson. Nelson Books and Thomas Nelson are registered trademarks of HarperCollins Christian Publishing, Inc.

Originally published in association with the literary agency of Wolgemuth & Associates, Inc. Original layout, design, and writing assistance by Gregory C. Benoit Publishing, Old Mystic, CT.

"Unleashing God's Truth, One Verse at a Time®" is a trademark of Grace to You. All rights reserved.

Thomas Nelson titles may be purchased in bulk for educational, business, fundraising, or sales promotional use. For information, please e-mail SpecialMarkets@ThomasNelson.com.

Scripture quotations are taken from *The New King James Version.* © 1982 by Thomas Nelson. Used by permission. All rights reserved.

Some material from the Introduction, "Keys to the Text" and "Exploring the Meaning" sections taken from *The MacArthur Bible Commentary,* John MacArthur, Copyright © 2005 Thomas Nelson Publishers.

ISBN 978–07180–3476–4

First Printing April 2016 / Printed in the United States of America

HB 05.01.2024

Contents

INTRODUCTION

The nation of Israel began as one unified state composed of twelve tribes of God's chosen people living in the Promised Land. Under King David, the nation had vanquished its enemies and found the blessing that God had promised them. But all that changed when David's son Solomon added pagan elements to the proper worship of the Lord and led Israel away from God's Word. God responded to this sin by dividing the nation in two.

The Lord left ten tribes in the north (who retained the name *Israel*) and two in the south (the tribes of Judah and Benjamin, who called themselves *Judah*). Israel would go on to experience a long line of ungodly kings, with each monarch seemingly more sinful than his predecessor. Judah, meanwhile, retained the line of David, and while that kingdom also experienced evil rulers, there were a number who followed in David's footsteps. In the midst of these tumultuous times, God sent prophets to both Israel and Judah, pleading with His people to turn away from their sin and return to fellowship with Him.

The books of Kings cover a period of more than 400 years, and during those years, as one would expect, there were great fluctuations in world power. Egypt and Assyria wrestled back and forth for dominance, until both were eventually overshadowed by Babylon (modern-day Iraq). Babylon itself would later be overshadowed by Persia (modern-day Iran). Ultimately, when the time of judgment arrived for God's people, the Lord would use Assyria to conquer Israel and Babylon to conquer Judah. In this way, both kingdoms came to an inglorious end.

In these twelve studies, we will examine the reign of kings depicted in the book of 2 Kings and witness the events that led to the demise of Israel and Judah. We will look at the godly reigns of some of Judah's kings (such as Jehoshaphat, Jehoash, and Hezekiah) and the wicked reigns of some of Israel's kings during its last days. We will also examine some of the individuals who stood against the idolatry that polluted Israel—prophets such as Elisha and priests such as Jehoiada—who stayed true to God's Word at risk of their own lives.

Through it all, we will learn some precious truths about the character of God, and we will see His great faithfulness in keeping His promises. We will learn, in short, what it means to follow God wholeheartedly and walk by faith.

TITLE

First and Second Kings were considered one book in the earliest Hebrew manuscripts. They were later divided into two books by the translators of the Greek version, known as the Septuagint. This division was later followed by the Latin Vulgate, English translations, and modern Hebrew Bibles. The earliest Hebrew manuscripts titled the one book *Kings*, after the first word in verse 1. The books of 1 and 2 Samuel and 1 and 2 Kings combined represent a chronicle of the entire history of Judah's and Israel's kingship from Saul to Zedekiah.

AUTHOR AND DATE

Jewish tradition proposed that Jeremiah wrote Kings. However, this is unlikely because Jeremiah never went to Babylon where the final event of the book takes place, and the date this event took place (561 BC) would have made him at least eighty-six years old at the time. Based on the fact 1 and 2 Kings emphasize the ministry of prophets, it seems likely it was written by an unnamed prophet who lived during the exile. The evidence seems to point to a single author living in Babylon who drew from pre-exilic source materials to complete the books.

The last narrated event in 2 Kings 25:27–30 sets the earliest possible date of completion, and because there is no record of the end of the Babylonian captivity in Kings, the Israelites' release from exile identifies the latest possible writing date. This sets the date for the works between 561–538 BC. This date is sometimes challenged on the basis of the "to this day" statements throughout the books, but it is best to understand these as coming from sources the author used rather than by the author himself.

BACKGROUND AND SETTING

The action in 1 and 2 Kings takes place in the whole land of Israel, from Dan to Beersheba, including the Transjordan. The author tells of four invading nations who played a dominant role in the affairs of Israel and Judah from 971 to 561 BC. The first was Egypt, who impacted Israel's history during the tenth century BC. The second was Syria (Aram), who posed a threat during the ninth century BC. The third was Assyria, who terrorized Palestine from the mid-eighth century to the late seventh century BC and ultimately destroyed the northern kingdom of Israel in 722 BC. The fourth was Babylon, who became the dominant power from 612 to 539 BC. The Babylonians destroyed Jerusalem in 586 BC, carrying the people of Judah into captivity.

The author of Kings, an exile in Babylon, wrote the book to communicate the lessons of Israel's history—from the ascension of Solomon in 971 BC to the destruction of Jerusalem in 586 BC—to the Jews living in exile. To accomplish this, he traced the histories of two sets of kings and two nations of disobedient people—Israel and Judah—to show how the people grew indifferent to God's law and His prophets. The sad reality he reveals is that all the kings of Israel and the majority of the kings of Judah were apostates who led their people into idolatry. Because of the kings' failure, God sent His prophets to confront the people with their sin. When this message was rejected, the people were ultimately carried into exile.

HISTORICAL AND THEOLOGICAL THEMES

The book of 2 Kings begins with the reign of King Ahaziah in Israel and King Joram/Jehoram in Judah and concludes with the decline and fall of both kingdoms. Each king is introduced with (1) his name and relation to his predecessor, (2) his date of accession, (3) his age in coming to the throne (for kings of Judah only), (4) his length of reign, (5) his place of reign, (6) his mother's name (for Judah only), and (7) the author's spiritual appraisal of his reign. This introduction is followed by a narration of the events that occurred during the reign of each king. Each reign is concluded with (1) a citation of sources, (2) additional historical notes, (3) notice of death, (4) notice of burial, (5) the name of the successor, and (6) in a few instances, an added postscript.

Three theological themes are emphasized in Kings. The first is that the Lord judged Israel and Judah because of their disobedience to His law. This unfaithfulness on the part of the rebellious people was furthered by the apostasy of the evil kings who led them into idolatry, which caused the Lord to exercise His righteous wrath against them.

A second theme is that the word of the true prophets always came to pass. Several times we are led to understand the narrated events happened "according to the word of the LORD which He had spoken by His servants the prophets" (2 Kings 24:2; see also 1 Kings 13:2–3; 22:15–28; 2 Kings 23:16). The Lord always kept His Word, even His warnings of judgment.

A third theme is that the Lord remembered His promise to David (see 1 Kings 11:12; 15:4; 2 Kings 8:19). Even though the kings of the Davidic line proved to be disobedient, God did not bring David's family to an end. Even as the book closes, the line of David still exists, so there is hope for the coming "seed" of David (see 2 Samuel 7:12–16).

INTERPRETIVE CHALLENGES

The major interpretive challenge in 1 and 2 Kings concerns the *chronology of the kings of Israel and Judah*. Although the author provides abundant chronological data in the books, this information is difficult to interpret for two reasons. First, there seems to be inconsistencies in the information given. For instance, 1 Kings 16:23 states that Omri, king of Israel, began to reign in the thirty-first year of Asa, king of Judah, and that he reigned twelve years. However, according to 1 Kings 16:29, Omri was succeeded by his son Ahab in the thirty-eighth year of Asa, giving Omri a reign of only seven years, not twelve.

Second, extrabiblical sources (Greek, Assyrian, and Babylonian) seem to provide contrasting dates to those given in 1 and 2 Kings. For instance, Ahab and Jehu, kings of Israel, are believed to be mentioned in Assyrian records. Based on these records, Ahab's death can be fixed at 853 BC, and Jehu's reign at

841 BC. With these dates, it is possible to determine the date of the division of Israel from Judah was c. 931 BC, the fall of Samaria was 722 BC, and the fall of Jerusalem was 586 BC. However, when the total years of royal reigns in 1 and 2 Kings are added, the number for Israel is 241 years (not 210) and for Judah is 393 years (not 346).

The solution to this problem is to recognize there were some co-regencies in both kingdoms—a period when two kings ruled at the same time—so the overlapping years were counted twice in the total for both kings. Further, different methods of reckoning the years of a king's rule and even different calendars were used at differing times in the two kingdoms, resulting in the seeming internal inconsistencies. The accuracy of the chronology in Kings can be demonstrated and confirmed.

A second major interpretive challenge deals with Solomon's relationship to the Abrahamic and Davidic covenants. Some interpret 1 Kings 4:20–21 as the fulfillment of the promises given to Abraham (see Genesis 15:18–21; 22:17). However, according to Numbers 34:6, the western border of the land promised to Abraham was the Mediterranean Sea. Furthermore, in 1 Kings 5:1, Hiram is an independent king of Tyre and deals with Solomon as an equal. Solomon's empire was not the fulfillment of the land promise given to Abraham by the Lord, though a great portion of that land was under Solomon's control.

Further, Solomon's statements in 1 Kings 5:5 and 8:20 seem to represent his claims to be the promised seed of the Davidic covenant, and the author of Kings holds out the possibility that Solomon's temple was the fulfillment of the Lord's promise to David. However, it is equally clear that Solomon did not meet the conditions required for the fulfillment of the promise to David (see 11:9–13). In fact, none of the historical kings in the house of David met the conditions of complete obedience that was to be the sign of the Promised One. The books of Kings thus point Israel to a future hope under the Messiah when the covenants would be fulfilled.

THE KINGS OF ISRAEL AND JUDAH (C. 853–586 BC)

King of Israel	Reign (BC)*	Length (years)
Ahaziah	853–852	2
Joram (Jehoram)	852–841	12
Jehu	841–814	28
Jehoahaz	814–798	17
Jehoash (Joash)	798–882	16
Jeroboam II	782 (793)–753	41
Zechariah	753–752	(6 months)
Shallum	752	(1 month)
Menahem	752–742	10
Pekahiah	742–740	2
Pekah	740 (752)–732	20
Hoshea	732–722	9
10 northern tribes enter captivity	722	

King of Judah	Reign (BC)*	Length (years)
Jehoshaphat	870 (873)–848	25
Jehoram (Joram)	848 (853)–841	8
Ahaziah (Jehoahaz)	841	1
Queen Athaliah	841–835	6
Joash (Jehoash)	835–796	40
Amaziah	796–767	29
Uzziah (Asariah)	767 (792)–740	52
Jotham	740 (750)–731	16
Ahaz	731 (735)–715	16
Hezekiah	715 (729)–686	29
Manasseh	686 (696)–642	55
Amon	642–640	2
Josiah	640–609	31
Jehoahaz (Shallum)	609	(3 months)
Jehoiakim (Eliakim)	609–598	11
Jehoiachin (Coniah)	598–597	(3 months)
Zedekiah (Mattaniah)	597–586	11
Judah enters captivity	586	

*All dates are approximate. Dates in parentheses indicate a co-regency of father and son.

THE KINGSHIP OF JEHOSHAPHAT

1 Kings 22:41–50

DRAWING NEAR

What does it mean to "lead by example"? Why is it important for godly leaders not only to set a good example but also instruct people in how to act and behave?

_____

_____

_____

THE CONTEXT

When King Asa died, his son Jehoshaphat took the throne in Judah. In fact, it is likely that Jehoshaphat reigned alongside his father as co-regent in Judah during the last years of Asa's life, when he was suffering from a severe disease in his feet (possibly gangrene). Although during Asa's final years he placed his faith in men rather than in God, his kingship had been mostly good, because Asa was generally a godly king.

His son, however, was even godlier. King Jehoshaphat was not perfect, of course, and he had a weakness for making bad alliances. One such alliance was with the wicked King Ahab who, together with his evil queen, Jezebel, had led Israel into idolatry and murdered God's prophets. Jehoshaphat had allied himself with Ahab by marrying his son to Ahab's daughter. He then joined with Ahab in a military alliance against Syria that almost cost him his life.

Nevertheless, Jehoshaphat's reign was characterized by godliness and obedience, and the Bible declares emphatically that he walked in the ways of David. Of course, one cannot teach God's Word without first living it out, but Jehoshaphat did this as well. As we will see in this study, when he was faced with a terrific crisis he did not rely on any of his human alliances but turned immediately to God for help—and the Lord did not let him down. We will learn, as did Jehoshaphat and the people of Judah, that the battle belongs to God, not to us.

KEYS TO THE TEXT

Read 1 Kings 22:41–50, noting the key words and phrases indicated below.

A GODLY KING: When Jehoshaphat takes the throne, he follows his father's godly example, leads Judah in the ways of the Lord, and teaches the people from God's Word.

22:41. JEHOSHAPHAT THE SON OF ASA: Jehoshaphat's name means "Jehovah has judged." The statement that he became king of Judah "in the fourth year of Ahab" refers to the beginning of Jehoshaphat's reign, after being co-regent with his father Asa (in 870 BC).

42. HE REIGNED TWENTY-FIVE YEARS: Jehoshaphat reigned from 873–848 BC. The author of Chronicles states he ruled Judah during turbulent times, when the nation faced enemies in every direction—including their own kinsmen of Israel immediately to the north. This was, therefore, prudent leadership, and the nation of Judah enjoyed a season of peace. It is important to note, however, that the peace was due to the neighboring nations experiencing "the fear of the LORD" (verse 10), not the fear of Judah's military might (see 2 Chronicles 17:2).

43. HE WALKED IN ALL THE WAYS OF HIS FATHER ASA: Jehoshaphat followed in his father Asa's footsteps and did what pleased the Lord. As we have

seen, the Lord promises to be with His people if they seek Him and observe His commands. This does not mean a person earns God's favor by doing good deeds, for God's favor cannot be earned by any person or by any means. Nevertheless, those who have been redeemed must live in fellowship with the Lord if they want to experience the full presence and blessing of God in their lives.

DOING WHAT WAS RIGHT: In 1 Chronicles 17:6 we read that "his heart took delight in the ways of the LORD," which could be literally translated "his soul was exalted." This suggests that Jehoshaphat found pleasure in obeying God's Word and that the process enriched his entire being. Interestingly, this was the first time the author described any king since the division of Israel and Judah as one who delighted in God's way.

44. MADE PEACE WITH THE KING OF ISRAEL: According to 2 Chronicles 19:2, Jehu the prophet rebuked Jehoshaphat for making this alliance with Ahaziah, the son of the wicked King Ahab who succeeded his father to the throne of Israel. Jehu said to Jehoshaphat, "Should you help the wicked and love those who hate the LORD? Therefore the wrath of the LORD is upon you." Ahaziah would end up reigning only two years over Israel (see 1 Kings 22:51).

45. THE REST OF THE ACTS OF JEHOSHAPHAT: In Chronicles 17:7, we read that one of these acts was to send leaders to teach in the cities of Judah. Asa had commanded the people of Judah to seek God, but Jehoshaphat went further and taught the people from God's Word. This was God's original intention for the leaders of Israel at every level: that they instruct others in the Word of God. Making God's commandments the law of the land forces a nation to live by godly principles, but teaching the people His Word permits them to love Him of their own free will.

45. AND HOW HE MADE WAR: The author of Chronicles goes into more detail about this war, which Jehoshaphat fought against Moab, Ammon, and other Canaanite tribes (see 2 Chronicles 20:1–30 and the Going Deeper section below).

47. NO KING IN EDOM: Jehoshaphat controlled the region of Edom, which gave him access to the seaport of Ezion Geber. He sought to emulate Solomon's fleet and wealth, but he was unsuccessful in doing so. According to 2 Chronicles 20:36–37, the Lord destroyed his fleet because of Jehoshaphat's agreement to build it with Ahaziah.

49. LET MY SERVANTS GO WITH YOUR SERVANTS: This apparently refers to a subsequent attempt by Ahaziah to continue the joint venture after the disaster.

GOING DEEPER

The author of Chronicles gives us some details about Jehoshaphat's reign not found in the book of Kings. Read 2 Chronicles 20:1–30, noting the key words and phrases indicated below.

> BETRAYAL: *After Jehoshaphat institutes his reforms, three armies suddenly attack the nation of Judah—nations the Israelites had historically treated well.*

20:1. THE PEOPLE OF MOAB WITH THE PEOPLE OF AMMON: These were Canaanite neighbors to the east of Judah and Israel, respectively. (See the map in the Introduction.)

3. JEHOSHAPHAT FEARED: In this case, fear was the normal human reaction to the grave threat that had suddenly materialized. But Jehoshaphat did not permit his fear to control him; instead, he immediately turned to the Lord for help.

SET HIMSELF TO SEEK THE LORD: King Jehoshaphat devoted himself to prayer and fasting, committing all his time and energy to calling on the Lord. As the king, he must have had many pressing concerns and obligations, and he certainly had urgent business to attend to with an invading army at his doorstep. However, Jehoshaphat set aside all those distractions and concentrated his heart and mind on prayer.

> JEHOSHAPHAT'S PRAYER: *The king comes before the Lord with an urgent plea and places the battle in God's hands.*

6. DO YOU NOT RULE OVER ALL THE KINGDOMS OF THE NATIONS: Jehoshaphat recognized that kings and rulers—even sinful ones—reign under the will and authority of God. God will judge sinful leaders for their actions, but in the end, a nation stands or falls solely according to God's will.

7. DROVE OUT THE INHABITANTS OF THIS LAND: The Lord had expelled the Canaanites from the Promised Land because they had devoted themselves to false gods. Israel was following the same course at this time, but under Jehoshaphat's leadership the nation of Judah had turned away from idolatry—for a time. In the end, both Israel and Judah would be driven out of Canaan for the same reason.

10. AMMON, MOAB, AND MOUNT SEIR: The Ammonites and Moabites were descendants of Lot (Abraham's nephew), and the descendants of Esau (Jacob's twin brother) lived in Mount Seir. The Lord had specifically instructed Israel not to fight against these nations when they were leaving Egypt for Canaan (see Deuteronomy 2), but to treat them with respect. Jehoshaphat was reminding the Lord in his prayer that Judah and Israel had gone out of their way to be at peace with these people, and now their kindness was being betrayed.

12. WE HAVE NO POWER: A recurring lesson for the people of Judah was to recognize they had no power in themselves to control the future or to subdue their enemies. The godly kings, such as Jehoshaphat, understood this and turned to the Lord for protection when threatened by destruction. But the ungodly kings, such as Rehoboam and Abijam, tried to solve their problems through their own strength—or worse, by turning to man-made idols. Jehoshaphat also understood that the first step in seeking God was to keep his eyes on Him. Today this is done by studying His Word, asking His will in prayer, and obeying His direction in daily action.

13. WITH THEIR LITTLE ONES, THEIR WIVES, AND THEIR CHILDREN: Walking with God is a family matter, and a believer's children should be included in the entire process. The Lord had commanded the Israelites to teach His Word to their children from their earliest years (see Deuteronomy 6:6–9), training them how to walk in obedience when they were young so they would have wisdom when they came to lead their own families.

THE LORD'S RESPONSE: *In response to Jehoshaphat's prayer, the Lord sends a prophet to the people of Judah to instruct them on what to do.*

15. DO NOT BE AFRAID NOR DISMAYED: Although fear is a natural response to danger, it can also become a debilitating danger in itself. God's Word frequently exhorts believers to resist fear and to be courageous. Jehoshaphat was afraid when he heard of the coming invasion, but he also demonstrated how one overcomes fear: by turning to the Lord in prayer.

THE BATTLE IS NOT YOURS, BUT GOD'S: Once again, the Lord reminded His people that He was their sole source of security against this world's threats. God wants His children to depend on Him for everything rather than on their own devices. This is not a passive process, however, for we must be actively walking in obedience and faith. The Lord frequently calls us to participate in His plans—but the ultimate direction and outcome of those plans are entirely in His hands.

16. GO DOWN AGAINST THEM: Here is an example of the above principle: the Lord had declared the battle was entirely His, yet He also wanted His people to be involved. They were not to sit at home, passively waiting for God to destroy their enemies. They had a role to play, and the Lord insisted they do their part.

THE ASCENT OF ZIZ . . . WILDERNESS OF JERUEL: These lie between En-Gedi on the Dead Sea and Tekoa, which is ten miles south of Jerusalem and seventeen miles northwest of En-Gedi. This is the pass that leads from the valley of the Dead Sea toward Jerusalem.

17. YOU WILL NOT NEED TO FIGHT: When believers turn the battle over to God's control, they gain an omniscient Commander in Chief. The Lord never needs to speculate or strategize, for He knows all things in advance. No human leader could ever hope to stand before God's wisdom and power.

POSITION YOURSELVES, STAND STILL AND SEE: Here is some practical instruction on how to turn a battle over to God's control. To position oneself is to take a deliberate and public stand, making a firm determination that one belongs to God. To stand still requires one to stop fighting and cease from one's own attempts to control or conquer. When believers determine to allow God to control a situation and stop fighting in their own power, they will invariably see God's faithfulness and sovereignty—and they will ultimately see great victory.

GO OUT AGAINST THEM: It is significant the Lord commanded His people to not fight and then commanded them to go out against the foe as though to war. It is true that the Lord would fight the battle, but again we see that the people of Judah had a part in the conflict. Their share in the battle was to stand firm and sing God's praises. It may have seemed an insignificant role to them, but it was an integral part of the battle plan nonetheless.

PREPARING FOR BATTLE: *As the people of Judah follow God's instructions and sing praises to Him, the Lord creates confusion among the ranks of their enemies.*

18. WORSHIPING THE LORD: This was an open act of faith, as the people of Judah praised and worshiped the Lord before the battle even began. God

had promised a victory and the people believed Him, knowing that He always keeps His promises.

19. WITH VOICES LOUD AND HIGH: The people's worship was open and public, and they didn't hold back in singing God's praises. This was a public testimony for the world around them as well as an encouragement to the people of Judah as they prepared to face a powerful foe.

21. THE BEAUTY OF HOLINESS: The Lord is beautiful in holiness (see Exodus 15:11), but the text here would better be translated "in holy attire," which was referring to the manner in which the Levite singers were clothed in sacred clothing in honor of the Lord's holiness.

22. THE LORD SET AMBUSHES: God might have sent angels to create confusion and mayhem among the enemy, or He might have simply used the natural distrust that these three nations had for one another. Ammon and Moab were descendants of Lot and thus a sort of national cousins, while Esau's descendants from Mount Seir were more like outsiders. However the Lord accomplished it, the rout was similar to His miraculous preservation of Israel during Gideon's day (see Judges 7).

24. THERE WERE THEIR DEAD BODIES: The people of Judah marched out to battle, but the war was over before they got there! They did not have to do anything but gather up the spoils.

28. TO THE HOUSE OF THE LORD: The ordeal ended where it began: at the house of God. The people of Judah did not forget to praise and thank the Lord for answering their prayers, which is an important step in our relationship with God as well.

UNLEASHING THE TEXT

1) What made Jehoshaphat a good king? How did his reign compare with that of his father, King Asa? How did it compare with Rehoboam's reign?

2) Why did Jehoshaphat send leaders into Judah to teach the people? How did this differ from Asa's approach? How is Jehoshaphat's approach superior?

_____

_____

_____

_____

3) Why did the prophet Jahaziel command the people to "not be afraid nor dismayed" (2 Chronicles 20:15)? How might fear have hindered the people of Judah from trusting God?

_____

_____

_____

_____

4) What did God mean when He commanded the people to position themselves, stand still, and see (see 2 Chronicles 20:17)? How are these things done?

_____

_____

_____

_____

EXPLORING THE MEANING

The battle belongs to God, but we also have a role to play. Jehoshaphat recognized that his people were powerless to defeat the terrible foe that came to destroy them, and he turned to the Lord for deliverance. This was exactly the right response, for the Lord wants His people to let Him fight their battles. God promised the king that He would rout the foe, "for the battle is not yours, but God's" (2 Chronicles 20:15).

Nevertheless, this promise did not give the people of Judah the right to go home and take a nap until the war was over. The Lord was indeed going to do the fighting for them, but they still had a part to play in the conflict. It was not an aggressive part—on the contrary, their role was to take a position, stand firm in it, and watch. Their task was to trust the Lord would keep His promises and then stand firm in that faith even though they were faced with an enemy that threatened to destroy them. By standing firm in their faith, they were free to watch for God's great deliverance—and when it came, they saw their faith was not in vain.

This is what it means to stand strong in the faith. We have the steadfast assurance that God will always keep His promises, and we can fully depend on Him to protect us and fight on our behalf against the enemy who seeks to destroy us. When we are firm in our faith, we can see God at work in our lives for His glory, and we can also realize that all the glory belongs to God. He will deliver us, and we will surely see that our faith is not in vain.

Obedience produces blessing. The Bible makes it clear that sin has negative consequences. When people live in sin, they incur not only divine chastisement and displeasure but also the temporal negative consequences of sin. However, obedience has consequences as well: it produces blessing in a person's life. As an example of this principle, the author of 2 Chronicles tells us "the LORD was with Jehoshaphat, because he walked in the former ways of his father David; he did not seek the Baals, but sought the God of his father, and walked in His commandments and not according to the acts of Israel" (17:3–4).

Jehoshaphat obeyed the Lord, and as a result he experienced the blessing of divine pleasure. It was not that Jehoshaphat's obedience *caused* God's blessing; rather, it would be more accurate to say that obedience came with

God's blessing. In other words, blessing was the result of Jehoshaphat's obedience. When people obey God, they experience not only divine approval but also the joy of walking with the Lord.

When we deliberately disregard God's commands, we cheat ourselves and hinder His work in our lives. Jesus taught, "If you keep My commandments, you will abide in My love, just as I have kept My Father's commandments and abide in His love" (John 15:10). When we abide in Jesus' love, we receive the fullness of the Father's blessings in our lives, and we grow ever more in Christ's image.

The godly leader teaches others from God's Word. Jehoshaphat's kingship, for the most part, was a model of godly leadership. His father, Asa, had commanded the people of Judah to observe and obey the Word of God, and this was good. But Jehoshaphat actively *instructed* the people in God's Word, and this was even better. He understood that while enforced obedience might cause a nation to outwardly obey God's commands, it did not cause an inward transformation of love and worship on the people's part. The first step in that process came from understanding the Word of God.

God calls each of us to various levels of authority—whether in the home, the church, the workplace, or the community—and He wants us to be teaching others from His Word. This is accomplished first and foremost through our example, and in this sense we have the authority to teach by example to the world around us. Yet our teaching should extend beyond outward obedience to include actively telling others the truth of Jesus Christ. This can be illustrated within a godly home, as parents—and especially fathers—are commanded by God to teach their children from God's Word on a regular basis.

Jesus, of course, is the perfect example of this principle. He lived a sinless life, completely obeying all that His Father commanded Him, and His life was a living epistle of God's truth to the world around. Yet Jesus did not stop with obedience—even perfect obedience. He coupled His walk with His words and openly taught God's truth to all who would listen. This is what Jesus commanded His disciples to do: "Go therefore and make disciples of all the nations . . . teaching them to observe all things that I have commanded you" (Matthew 28:19–20). The godly leader will follow Jesus' example, both living and teaching the Word of God.

REFLECTING ON THE TEXT

5) What does it mean that Jehoshaphat's "heart took delight in the ways of the LORD" (2 Chronicles 17:6)? How is this done? What are the results?

_____

_____

_____

_____

6) What role did music and praise play in the battle God fought on behalf of Judah? What role did worship play? How are these things important to resting in faith?

_____

_____

_____

_____

7) In your own words, what exactly does it mean to stand strong in the faith? How is this done? What are the results?

_____

_____

_____

_____

8) What godly teachers have influenced your life? How did they couple godly behavior with teaching by word? How might you imitate their examples?

_____

_____

_____

PERSONAL RESPONSE

9) What battles is the Lord calling you to turn over to Him at present? How will you do that? What steps will you take this week to rest in faith?

_____

_____

_____

10) Is there an area of deliberate disobedience in your life? If so, what will you do today to turn away from that sinful behavior?

_____

_____

_____

2

ELISHA TAKES THE MANTLE

2 Kings 1:1–2:25

DRAWING NEAR

What makes for a successful transition of power from one leader to another in politics? What makes for a successful transition of power within the church?

_____

_____

_____

THE CONTEXT

The book of 1 Kings ends with the death of the wicked King Ahab of Israel, who was struck by an arrow shot by a random soldier during a battle against Syria. Ahab had tried to thwart God's prophecies predicting his death by wearing a disguise, but God was not fooled, and the "dogs licked up his blood" (1 Kings 22:38). The rule of Israel then fell to Ahab's son Ahaziah, who continued to promote Baal worship. The Lord quickly brought an end to his reign, after only two years, when Ahaziah was mortally wounded after falling from the roof of his palace.

Ahaziah had no heir, so the throne went to his younger brother, Joram (also spelled Jehoram). Like his father, he did evil in God's sight, though he did remove an image of Baal that King Ahab had set up in the temple (see 2 Kings 3:2). (Note the king of Judah at this time, the son of Jehoshaphat, was also named Jehoram/Joram.) Israel's old enemy Syria was still actively working to destroy God's people, and while the two nations were not engaged in an all-out war, Syria was continually carrying out raids and skirmishes on Israel's soil.

Meanwhile, Elijah had grown old in service to the Lord, and the time of his departure was at hand. But by "departure" we do not mean death, for the Lord had revealed to Elijah that he would not die but would instead be translated directly into heaven, in bodily form. His servant Elisha was already appointed by God to carry on his mentor's great ministry, yet Elisha may have felt some concern about his ability to walk in Elijah's footsteps. He lived in troubled times, and he may well have felt inadequate to the daunting task ahead.

Nevertheless, Elisha knew where Elijah's power came from, and he made a bold final request of his mentor before their parting: a double portion of Elijah's spirit. As we will see in this study, the Lord granted his request and demonstrated His mighty power in dramatic ways.

Keys to the Text

Read 2 Kings 1:1–2:25, noting the key words and phrases indicated below.

> THE KINGS TAKES A FALL: *King Ahaziah is on his roof one day when the lattice gives way and he falls to the ground below. He sends a messenger to ask his god, Baal, if he will recover.*

1:2. LATTICE OF HIS UPPER ROOM: King Ahaziah's rooftop room was enclosed with crossbars of interwoven reed or wood strips, which shut out direct sunlight while letting in cool breezes. For reasons not explained in the text, it was not sturdy enough to keep him from falling.

INQUIRE OF BAAL-ZEBUB: Baal-Zebub means "lord of the flies," which suggests he was the storm god who controlled diseases brought by flies. The name may have also been the sarcastic Israelite parody of Baal-Zebul, meaning "prince Baal" or "exalted lord," a common title for Baal. The New Testament writers preserved the name in the form *Beelzebul*, a name for Satan, the prince of the demons (see Matthew 10:25; Mark 3:22; Luke 11:15).

3. THE ANGEL OF THE LORD: Some interpret this as a reference to the preincarnate Christ, but it is probably to an angelic messenger, like the one sent earlier by the Lord to Elijah (see 1 Kings 19:7). The Lord's messenger was in contrast to the messengers of the wicked king.

ELIJAH THE TISHBITE: The record of this unusual prophet to Israel began in 1 Kings 17:1 and extends to 2 Kings 2:11. The term "Tishbite" refers to his place of birth, Tishbe, which was probably located in the upper Galilee region.

THE DEATH OF AHAZIAH: Ahaziah has inquired of Baal regarding his injuries, but it is the Lord God who gives him the news that he will not recover from his wounds.

4. YOU SHALL SURELY DIE: The Lord's punishment on Ahaziah for consulting a false god instead of Yahweh was that he would fail to recover from his injuries. This was a merciful application of the Mosaic Law, which demanded death (see Exodus 22:20).

8. A HAIRY MAN: This phrase can be interpreted either to mean that Elijah was physically hairy or that he wore a garment made of hair, though the language supports the second viewpoint. Elijah likely wore a coarse wool garment girded at the waist with a leather belt.

9. MAN OF GOD: A technical title for a man who spoke for God.

10. FIRE CAME DOWN FROM HEAVEN: This was the proof that Elijah was a prophet of the Lord and entitled to respect. Additionally, it was an indication that Elijah was like Moses, whom the Lord also validated as His prophet by fire from heaven (see Numbers 16:35).

17. JEHORAM BECAME KING . . . JEHORAM THE SON OF JEHOSHAPHAT: The first Jehoram mentioned (who we will refer to as Joram) was a son of Ahab, who ruled over the northern kingdom of Israel for twelve years (c. 852–841 BC). The second Jehoram mentioned was the son and successor to Jehoshaphat, who ruled in the southern kingdom of Judah (c. 853–841 BC).

SECOND YEAR: This was the second year of Jehoram of Judah's co-regency with Jehoshaphat, his father (c. 852 BC).

ELIJAH'S FAREWELL TOUR: Elijah is nearing the end of his ministry. He and Elisha travel to the schools of prophets one more time so Elijah can say goodbye.

2:1. ELIJAH WENT WITH ELISHA: The Lord had directed Elijah to appoint Elisha as his successor. He was to train Elisha to take his mantle of leadership—quite literally, as it turned out—and prepare him to be a prophet to God's people during a time of growing apostasy.

2. STAY HERE: Elijah made this request of Elisha three times, and three times Elisha steadfastly refused. It is possible that Elijah was merely suggesting that Elisha remain and minister at one of the schools of prophets, which would have permitted Elijah to depart alone. What Elijah discovered was that Elisha was determined to take on his mentor's difficult and lonely ministry. Elisha needed to be present when Elijah was taken to heaven if he were to receive a double portion of God's Spirit, yet Elijah also knew the cost of his ministry. Elisha showed that he was prepared to pay that cost.

3. TAKE AWAY: The same term was used of Enoch's translation to heaven (see Genesis 5:24). The question from the sons of the prophets implied that the Lord had revealed Elijah's imminent departure to them.

I KNOW; KEEP SILENT: Elisha's stern response indicates the Lord had also revealed this to him. It is possible the sons of the prophets had been expressing some excitement at knowing what was going to happen. If so, Elisha felt such voyeurism was inappropriate, for this was a day of sadness. Elisha was undoubtedly heavyhearted at the prospect of saying goodbye to his beloved teacher and friend, and any lighthearted chatter would have been unwelcome.

CROSSING THE JORDAN: Elisha refuses to leave Elijah's side, and so the two travel to the Jordan River. There the Lord miraculously parts the waters.

8. STRUCK THE WATER: Moses had similarly struck the Nile River with his rod when the Israelites were still in Egypt, turning the water to blood (see Exodus 7:14–25). This was a public demonstration that God's power was with Elijah. Elisha would later use this same demonstration of God's power (see verse 14).

9. A DOUBLE PORTION: Elisha was asking for the spiritual birthright, comparable to the double portion of inheritance that went to a man's firstborn

son. He was essentially asking to become Elijah's spiritual successor as leader of the prophets and a spokesman for God. It is interesting that the Bible records twice as many miracles through Elisha as through Elijah, but this was not what Elisha was requesting. His main concern was that he needed Elijah's mighty power if he was going to accomplish what the Lord was calling him to do.

10. YOU HAVE ASKED A HARD THING: Elijah's life was hard. He was persecuted, arrested, scorned, abused, and hated by the people. This was not a life that Elijah wanted someone he loved to have to endure. Moreover, Elijah himself was powerless to grant Elisha's request. He knew that if the Lord intended to say yes to Elisha, He would permit him to witness Elijah's ascent to heaven as a sign.

CHARIOTS OF FIRE: *The two prophets are deep in conversation when suddenly the Lord's messengers appear and carry Elijah to heaven.*

11. AS THEY CONTINUED ON AND TALKED: The Lord's appearing to whisk away Elijah was sudden and without warning, even though both of the prophets were expecting it. In the same way, the Lord Himself will descend with a shout to catch up His people from the earth, taking all believers to be with Him forever (see 1 Thessalonians 4:16–17). This is a stunning picture of how God can take His children from the earth.

A CHARIOT OF FIRE: The horse-drawn chariot was the fastest means of transport and the most powerful weapon of warfare in Elijah's day. The most fearsome chariots were made of wood, reinforced with iron, and generally drawn by a team of trained warhorses. But God's chariot and horses were made of fire, which gave a vivid picture to Elisha that His power and majesty exceeded anything the world was capable of producing.

ELIJAH WENT UP BY A WHIRLWIND INTO HEAVEN: We are not told why the Lord chose to take Elijah bodily into heaven in this way without experiencing death, yet a whirlwind and chariot of fire provided an apt conclusion to Elijah's fiery ministry.

12. THE CHARIOT OF ISRAEL AND ITS HORSEMEN: Israel's strength and welfare lay in God's hands, not in the nation's military might. God was taking away His representative from Israel, and Elisha knew that a nation without God's leadership was left defenseless. The Lord was not removing His prophets entirely, however, as Elisha would soon demonstrate.

TAKING THE MANTLE: Once the prophet Elijah has been taken up into heaven, Elisha picks up his mantle and assumes his role as a major prophet in Israel.

13. THE MANTLE OF ELIJAH: There was nothing unusual about Elijah's cloak. Elisha's use of it merely identified him to the sons of the prophets as Elijah's successor.

14. WHERE IS THE LORD GOD OF ELIJAH: Elisha was asking God to fulfill His promise, imbuing him with His Spirit, as He had for Elijah. It was not a lack of faith that prompted these words, but a public declaration that all miracles were from the hand of the Lord and that he had been ordained as Elijah's successor.

15. BOWED TO THE GROUND: This action symbolized the submission of the sons of the prophets to the preeminence of Elisha as the major prophet in Israel.

16. LET THEM GO AND SEARCH: The sons of the prophets had not seen Elijah's miraculous, physical ascension into heaven as Elisha had, so they naturally assumed Elijah had died and left his body behind. If that had been the case, it would have been a disgraceful disrespect for the great prophet to leave his body unburied. However, Elisha knew that Elijah had been taken to heaven without dying, so he told the others that their search would be futile.

17. THEY URGED HIM TILL HE WAS ASHAMED: That is, the sons of the prophets wore Elisha down with their continued importunate insistence. Elisha finally gave in and allowed them to search for Elijah, though he knew the search for the prophet's body would prove fruitless.

HEALING THE WATERS: The school of prophets in Jericho has no drinkable water. Elisha instructs the people to bring him a bowl with salt so the brook may be healed.

18. JERICHO: The Lord had destroyed the city of Jericho many years earlier when the Israelites first entered the Promised Land under the leadership of Joshua. At that time, the Lord had pronounced a curse on the destroyed city, declaring that anyone who attempted to rebuild it would do so at the cost of his sons' lives (see Joshua 6:26). This curse had been fulfilled just a few years prior to this event when a man named Hiel attempted to rebuild Jericho and had lost two sons in the process (see 1 Kings 16:34).

20. A NEW BOWL, AND PUT SALT IN IT: Here again we find Elisha calling for a clean vessel in which to work the Lord's miracle. The use of salt from a new jar symbolized the cleansing of the waters that God would miraculously do. The healing of Jericho's water, through Elisha, freed the city from Joshua's curse, making it habitable for humans once again.

21. NO MORE DEATH OF BARRENNESS: Only by God's will alone can death be eliminated and life be restored.

22. THE WATER REMAINS HEALED: Similarly, Christ's victory over death was absolute and final. When He establishes His eternal kingdom, there shall never again be any sin or death anywhere for all eternity.

UNLEASHING THE TEXT

1) Why did Elijah instruct Elisha to stay behind while he traveled from city to city? Why were the servants talking about Elijah's departure? Why did Elisha ask them to stop?

_____

_____

_____

_____

2) What did Elisha mean when he requested a "double portion" of Elijah's spirit? Why did he desire such a thing?

_____

_____

_____

_____

3) Read Joshua 6:26, followed by 1 Kings 16:34. What significance did Elisha's act have in regard to God's healing something that had once been subject to a curse?

_____

_____

_____

4) What did Elisha mean when he cried out, "My father, my father, the chariot of Israel and its horsemen" (2 Kings 2:12)?

_____

_____

_____

EXPLORING THE MEANING

God is jealous for our loyalty to Him. When King Ahaziah chose to consult Baal about his injuries, God's reaction was strong and severe. Through the prophet Elijah, God interrupted the trek and told Ahaziah's messengers the king would die because of his disloyalty to God. God took Ahaziah's faithlessness seriously, and his sin resulted in the deaths of two companies of soldiers and their captains (see 2 Kings 1:10–12).

The captain of the third group took a different approach: he acknowledged that Elijah spoke for God and humbly begged for mercy for the lives of himself and his men. God's response shows that when people give him the honor and respect He is due, He will show mercy. Yet He remains uncompromising in His demand that His people be completely loyal to Him. The Lord God will not share the hearts of His people with anyone or anything. As He said to the Israelites in the wilderness, "You shall worship no other god, for the LORD, whose name is Jealous, is a jealous God" (Exodus 34:14).

God wants all of our hearts—wholly devoted to Him—and He will do whatever it takes to show us He is worthy of His demand for complete honor and respect. He will show mercy where hearts are soft toward Him, but He will be uncompromising toward those whose hearts refuse to bend—removing those cancers that threaten to compromise the faith of others. Our God is not small, indecisive, or worried about hurting our feelings; rather, He is powerful, jealous for our loyalty, and generous in His rewards when we give it to Him.

The Lord will return one day. Elijah was one of only two men in the Bible who were taken to heaven without dying. His dramatic ascension in a whirlwind, accompanied by a chariot of fire and horses, demonstrated that God has absolute command over all the forces of nature, including death. It seemed utterly impossible to those left behind that a man might escape death, and the Scriptures tell us clearly that "it is appointed for men to die once" (Hebrews 9:27). Yet they searched and found no body of Elijah, for there was none to find.

We are not told why God chose to do this for Elijah, yet part of His reason was to present a clear demonstration to His people that He is able to whisk them into His presence suddenly, in the twinkling of an eye. The Bible promises this very thing will happen one day when "the Lord Himself will descend from heaven with a shout, with the voice of an archangel, and with the trumpet of God. . . . Then we who are alive and remain shall be caught up . . . in the clouds to meet the Lord in the air" (1 Thessalonians 4:16–17).

Just as Elijah and Elisha lived as messengers of God and walked in faithfulness to Him, Paul stated that he would be rewarded with a crown of righteousness from the Lord. What's more, Paul said this crown would also be awarded to "all who have loved His appearing" (2 Timothy 4:8). For the person who walks in faithfulness to Jesus Christ, His return to earth is a sight to be longed for and desired. Skeptics may doubt the Lord can take someone from the earth miraculously and without experiencing death, but Elijah's departure is an encouragement for us to long for the Lord's coming.

God makes us His heirs through Christ. Elisha's request to inherit a double portion of Elijah's spirit is significant. His request was the equivalent of asking to be made Elisha's spiritual heir, his firstborn, responsible for carrying on the ministry that God had given to Elijah. In biblical times, the firstborn son was always the successor of the head of a family, and he received all the status and power that accompanied that position. Note that Elisha didn't make this request out of a desire for power, but because he knew the work ahead would require it. The Bible records twice as many miracles performed through Elisha than through Elijah.

Believers in Christ, having received the adoption of the Spirit, are given this same status as heirs. As Paul wrote, "For as many as are led by the Spirit of God, these are sons of God. For you did not receive the spirit of bondage again to fear, but you received the Spirit of adoption by whom we cry out, 'Abba, Father'" (Romans 8:14–15). Furthermore, Jesus promises that when we take on His mantle, we will do even greater works than He performed (see John 14:12).

Like the prophet Elisha, we face a world today in which people have turned their hearts from God. Just like Elisha, we need a "double portion" of God's power to fulfill the great commission He has given to us to share the good news of Christ with a lost and hurting world. God provides this power in abundance to us through the gift of the Holy Spirit dwelling within us. As Jesus said to His followers, "You shall receive power when the Holy Spirit has come upon you; and you shall be witnesses" (Acts 1:8).

REFLECTING ON THE TEXT

5) How did God respond to Ahaziah's desire to seek the counsel of Baal-Zebub? What does this tell you about God's desires for our loyalty?

_____

_____

_____

6) In what ways did Elijah's ascension to heaven picture the rapture of Christ's church? How did it differ from the coming rapture?

_____

_____

_____

7) In what ways do people strive to live with hearts divided between God and this world? What keeps people from being wholeheartedly devoted to God?

_____

_____

_____

8) How have you seen God respond to those who humbly acknowledge their need before Him? How is God's mercy part of His holy character?

_____

_____

_____

PERSONAL RESPONSE

9) If Jesus returned today, what would He find you doing? How should His imminent return affect your life this week?

_____

_____

_____

10) In what ways has your heart been tempted to be divided? How can you rely on the power of God to help you be part of fulfilling His great commission?

_____

_____

_____

MINISTRY OF ELISHA

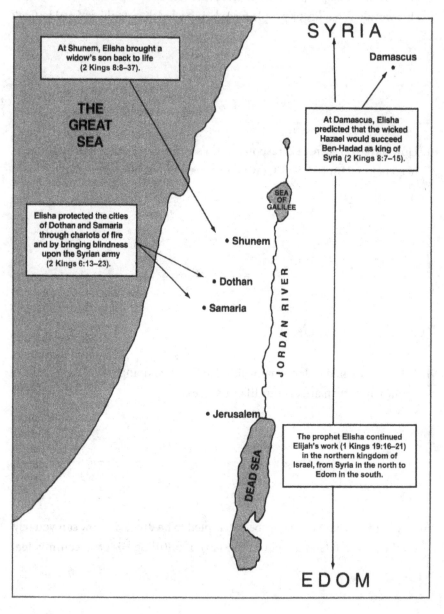

SYRIA

Damascus

At Shunem, Elisha brought a
widow's son back to life
(2 Kings 8:8–37).

THE
GREAT
SEA

At Damascus, Elisha
predicted that the wicked
Hazael would succeed
Ben-Hadad as king of
Syria (2 Kings 8:7–15).

SEA
OF
GALILEE

Elisha protected the cities
of Dothan and Samaria
through chariots of fire
and by bringing blindness
upon the Syrian army
(2 Kings 6:13–23).

• Shunem

• Dothan

JORDAN RIVER

• Samaria

• Jerusalem

The prophet Elisha continued
Elijah's work (1 Kings 19:16–21)
in the northern kingdom of
Israel, from Syria in the north to
Edom in the south.

DEAD SEA

EDOM

3

GOD'S MIRACULOUS PROVISION

2 Kings 4:1–44

DRAWING NEAR

What are some characteristics of people who practice generosity? What are some characteristics of people who practice hospitality?

_____

_____

_____

THE CONTEXT

Israel had fallen into Baal worship under Ahab, and that practice continued under the reign of Ahaziah. God had judged this king after he fell from his roof and sent messengers to inquire of Baal as to whether he would recover. The Lord had said to him, "You shall not come down from the bed to which you have gone up, but you shall surely die" (2 Kings 1:3–4).

This message to Ahaziah came through the mouth of Elijah, a bold and fiery man who confronted the people everywhere—from commoner to king—with the truth of God. Previously, he had squared off against 450 prophets of Baal on Mount Carmel, where God had miraculously sent fire to consume a water-soaked altar in answer to his prayers (see 1 Kings 18:20–40). After this, God sent Elijah to find Elisha, who had now literally picked up the mantle of his mentor and assumed his role as prophet in Israel.

Yet there were other men as well who preached the Word of God through-out Israel and Judah. Many of these men, known as the "sons of the prophets," had been trained in centers set up by Elijah and Elisha throughout the land. There were also common people throughout the land who supported the work of the prophets by providing them with a place to stay and food to eat. Often, as we have seen, they did this at great personal risk to themselves.

In today's study we will meet one such couple who supported Elisha in his ministry. This couple knew that Elisha made regular trips through the region, tracing a route that took him past their home, and decided to provide him with a "home away from home." Through their example, we learn not only how God provides for those who serve Him, but also how He works in their lives in miraculous ways.

KEYS TO THE TEXT

Read 2 Kings 4:1–44, noting the key words and phrases indicated below.

THE FLASK OF OIL: A widow approaches Elisha, asking for help in paying an overwhelming debt. God meets her need in overflowing abundance.

4:1. THE SONS OF THE PROPHETS: This was the group of prophets in training who met together for worship and fellowship as they sought to serve the Lord.

YOUR SERVANT MY HUSBAND IS DEAD: According to Jewish tradition, this prophet was Obadiah, who had served the Lord while also working in the court of King Ahab and Queen Jezebel. Jewish writings claim that he had borrowed money to feed the prophets of God when he hid them in caves to preserve their lives from Jezebel's murderous schemes.

THE CREDITOR IS COMING: It is likely that the widow incurred this debt as a result of how her husband cared for the prophets. In ancient times, people in debt could not only lose their property but also be taken into slavery for a time. The period of servitude could last until the next year of Jubilee (see Leviticus 25:39–40). Rich people and creditors, however, were not to take advantage of the destitute (see Deuteronomy 15:1–18).

2. A JAR OF OIL: This was probably olive oil, which could be used for either food or anointing wounds. It was not an expensive kind of oil.

3. BORROW VESSELS FROM EVERYWHERE: Elijah performed a similar miracle (see 1 Kings 17).

4. SHUT THE DOOR BEHIND YOU: The widow's need was private, so the provision for that need was to be private as well. Further, the absence of Elisha demonstrated that the miracle happened only by God's power. God's power multiplied little into much, filling all the vessels to meet the widow's need.

7. SELL THE OIL: The Lord had blessed the widow far beyond her need. The oil not only paid off her debt in full but also provided enough to support her and her sons for a long time afterward.

A HOSPITABLE WOMAN: A couple devotes themselves to serving God's prophet Elisha by providing an upper room for him to use whenever he is in the area.

8. ELISHA WENT TO SHUNEM: This town was in the territory of Issachar near Jezreel, on the slopes of Mount Moreh, overlooking the eastern end of the Jezreel Valley. The woman was evidently great in wealth and in social prominence.

9. MAN OF GOD: The woman recognized that Elisha was a prophet uniquely separated to God. His holiness prompted the woman to ask her husband to provide a separate, small, walled upper room for the prophet's personal use. The woman must have feared the "holy" Elisha coming into contact with their "profane" room.

10. A SMALL UPPER ROOM ON THE WALL: Ancient cities were often surrounded by thick walls where small apartments could be built. However, this phrase is probably better translated "a walled room on the roof." Typical homes in ancient Israel had flat roofs that were used in many capacities by the family, but they generally did not have separate rooms that were walled off from the rest of the rooftop. The Shunammite couple went to some expense and effort to remodel their home in order to provide Elisha with his own separate living quarters.

LET US PUT A BED FOR HIM THERE: This godly couple did not hold back on their hospitality to God's prophet but effectively created for him a private apartment within their home. This would have permitted Elisha to be part of their family for meals while still maintaining his independence and privacy for rest on his journeys. He could come and go as he needed without ever imposing on his hosts.

11. HE TURNED IN TO THE UPPER ROOM: This again suggests that Elisha had complete freedom within the home and could come and go without disturbing the couple. The house was probably built around a square central courtyard that had a staircase going up to the roof. Elisha may have simply entered the house and gone straight up to his apartment.

A GRATEFUL GUEST: Elisha demonstrates his gratitude to the woman by asking how the Lord can bless her, but she is content with her life and has no immediate needs.

12. GEHAZI HIS SERVANT: This man is described as Elisha's servant, but it would be more accurate to think of him as a protégé—a prophet in training—with Elisha as his mentor. Elisha enjoyed the same relationship with Elijah, though Gehazi would prove to have a vastly different character from Elisha.

CALL THIS SHUNAMMITE WOMAN: Elisha was not being aloof in sending Gehazi to call the woman but was likely seeing whether she was available to speak with him. Elisha also seems to have been giving Gehazi opportunities to minister to people to groom him for the Lord's work and thus mature in his service to God.

13. WHAT CAN I DO FOR YOU: Elisha recognized his hosts had gone to some trouble and expense on his behalf and, in a spirit of gratitude, wanted to do something for them in return. God calls His people to be both generous hosts and grateful guests.

SPEAK ON YOUR BEHALF TO THE KING: Elisha evidently had access to the king's presence, and he offered to intercede for the couple on any legal matter they might have faced. This couple was wealthy and lived in a remote area, so bandits were always a danger. Elisha was in effect offering to make sure they were protected by the military.

I DWELL AMONG MY OWN PEOPLE: The woman's response was basically, "I am content with my lot in life." She understood a fundamental principle of godliness, which is to learn to be content where the Lord has placed you.

GEHAZI'S IDEA: Elisha is still pondering what he can ask God to give this Shunammite woman when his servant Gehazi comes up with an intriguing idea.

14. WHAT THEN IS TO BE DONE FOR HER: This interaction between Elisha and Gehazi sheds some light on their relationship, which will be useful in a later study. They were conferring together to think up a suitable way of thanking the woman for her great hospitality.

SHE HAS NO SON: Gehazi's remark implied that the woman suffered the shame of being a barren woman and that her husband might die without an heir to carry on his name. In this time in Israel's history, a childless woman was sometimes viewed as being under God's judgment, and the woman would have keenly felt this sense of unwarranted shame.

16. DO NOT LIE TO YOUR MAIDSERVANT: Elisha's promise touched a deep nerve in the woman's heart, and she recoiled from being deluded with false hopes for something that she longed for so intensely. Her reply indicated that she felt having a son was impossible.

17. BUT THE WOMAN CONCEIVED: The Shunammite woman had been barren for many years, and her husband was old and past the normal time of fertility. However, as we have seen through these studies, God's power is not limited by natural circumstances or timetables, and He never fails to keep His word. After He promised a son to the woman through His prophet Elisha, He faithfully delivered. This unnamed woman joined the ranks of other women who gave birth miraculously, including Sarah, Hannah, and, most notably, Mary.

A TRAGIC DEATH: The woman has a son just as the Lord promised. However, sometime later the boy is out in the fields when he is stricken with an illness, and he dies in his mother's lap.

19. MY HEAD, MY HEAD: It is traditionally assumed that the young boy died of sunstroke, though that is not common among people who are accustomed to desert regions. (The cries of the boy, the body part affected, and the season of the year lead to that conclusion.) Other maladies have been suggested, but the exact cause of the tragedy remains uncertain.

21. LAID HIM ON THE BED OF THE MAN OF GOD: By placing her son's body on Elisha's bed, this woman showed that she had faith that Elisha's God could raise him from the dead, just as Elijah had done for another widow's son many years earlier (see 1 Kings 17).

22. THAT I MAY RUN TO THE MAN OF GOD: The mother of the boy apparently concealed the death of the child from her husband to spare him unnecessary grief, in light of the power of the man of God whom she believed might do a miracle for the boy.

23. NEITHER THE NEW MOON NOR THE SABBATH: In Elisha's day, the first day of the month and the seventh day of the week were marked with special religious observances and rest from work (see Numbers 28:9–15). The husband implied that only on such dates would a person visit a prophet.

25. MOUNT CARMEL: This was the site of Elijah's famous confrontation with the false prophets of Baal many years earlier (see 1 Kings 18). The distance from Shunem was approximately fifteen to twenty-five miles, or roughly a full day's journey.

26. IT IS WELL: The woman withheld the real sorrow of her son's death, waiting to tell the prophet Elisha directly.

27. SHE CAUGHT HIM BY THE FEET: This was a gesture both of extreme need and complete reliance on the man of God.

THE LORD HAS HIDDEN IT FROM ME: Elisha's great powers of insight and miracles were not due to some psychic ability or magical strength. On the contrary, he was a man, and he depended completely on the power and revelation of God.

GOD'S POWER OVER DEATH: The Lord demonstrates His complete sovereignty, even over death, by raising the son back to life.

29. LAY MY STAFF ON THE FACE OF THE CHILD: Elisha sent Gehazi ahead because he was younger and, therefore, faster than he was. He may have expected the Lord to restore the child's life when his staff was placed on him, in a way viewing that staff as representative of his own presence and a symbol of divine power.

31. THE CHILD HAS NOT AWAKENED: Elisha correctly understood that God could use any method He chose to perform His work. A Roman centurion would later come to understand this when he asked Jesus to heal his distant servant simply by speaking (see Matthew 8:5–13). In this present case, however, the Lord chose to work in other ways.

34. STRETCHED HIMSELF OUT ON THE CHILD: Much as Elijah had done in 1 Kings 17, Elisha demonstrated the Lord's power over death by raising the

couple's son from the dead. Also, like Elijah, part of the restoration process involved Elisha lying on top of the boy's body.

> FEEDING THE PEOPLE: *God performs two more miracles through the prophet Elisha: purifying a pot of stew and feeding one hundred men.*

38. ELISHA RETURNED TO GILGAL: This town was located about forty miles south of Shunem.

39. A LAPFUL OF WILD GOURDS: This was probably a kind of wild cucumber that could be fatally poisonous if eaten in large quantities.

41. BRING SOME FLOUR: Like Elijah before him, Elisha used flour to demonstrate God's concern for His people. The flour itself did not make the noxious stew edible, but God accomplished a miraculous cure through it.

42. BREAD OF THE FIRSTFRUITS: Normally, the firstfruits were reserved for God (see Leviticus 23:20) and the Levitical priests (see Numbers 18:13; Deuteronomy 18:4–5). Although the religion in the northern kingdom was apostate, the man who brought the loaves to Elisha was a representative of godly religion in Israel.

44. THEY ATE AND HAD SOME LEFT OVER: The multiplication of the loaves in accordance with the word of the Lord through His prophet Elisha anticipated the messianic ministry of Jesus Himself (see Matthew 14:16–20; 15:36–37; John 6:11–13).

UNLEASHING THE TEXT

1) Elisha instructed the poor widow in debt to close the door to her house. Why didn't he want this miracle to be seen by everyone?

_____

_____

_____

_____

2) What can we learn about God from the way He met the widow's needs? What does this reveal about God's dealings with Christians as individuals?

_____

_____

_____

3) Why did the couple from Shunem construct a special room for Elisha in their house? How did this help Elisha? How did it help the couple? What did it cost the couple?

_____

_____

_____

4) Why did the Shunammite woman lay her son's body on Elisha's bed? Why did she go to Elisha without telling her husband what had happened? Why wasn't Elisha able to do anything from up on Mount Carmel?

_____

_____

_____

EXPLORING THE MEANING

When we are most needy, God is most gracious. In this chapter in 2 Kings we read of five situations of dire need: (1) the widow who was on the verge of starvation, (2) the barren woman, (3) the grieving mother, (4) the poisoned stew, and (5) the men on the brink of starvation. In each of these situations, God met the need with His gracious provision. This stresses the fact that our God is a gracious God who loves to meet His people's needs.

However, when we rely on our wealth or find our joy in our possessions, we miss out the fact that God is capable of meeting our needs in this way. Often we are unable to see and appreciate the graciousness of God unless we first appreciate the depth of our needs. After all, the person who has never experienced hunger does not appreciate the ability of God to miraculously provide food. In times of our greatest need, not only must we turn to God for provision, but we must also recognize how He is meeting that need.

This same principle applies to our spiritual condition. Only when we realize the depth of our sin can we realize the graciousness of God in salvation. Only when we see how unable we are to save ourselves can we see how gracious God is. This is what Jesus meant when He said, "Those who are well have no need of a physician, but those who are sick. I have not come to call the righteous, but sinners, to repentance" (Luke 5:31–32).

God's people are called to be hospitable. The Shunammite woman set an excellent example of hospitality. She knew that Elisha, the Lord's servant, was making regular trips throughout the northern tribes of Israel, tracing a route that took him past her home periodically. She saw a need and met it by providing Elisha with a home away from home. This provision was costly to her and her husband, both financially and personally. They remodeled their home at cost to themselves and opened up their lives by sharing meals with God's servant.

The book of Hebrews reminds us that we, too, are to share with complete strangers: "Do not forget to entertain strangers, for by so doing some have unwittingly entertained angels" (2 Kings 13:2). In Genesis 18, we read of a time when Abraham entertained angels—and even the Lord Himself in a preincarnate appearance. Three strangers arrived at Abraham's camp, and he leaped up to welcome them and to prepare a sumptuous meal for them, little knowing at the time whom he was entertaining. He was tremendously blessed for his hospitality, as the Lord shared His plans for the coming judgment on Sodom and Gomorrah. If Abraham had not been hospitable, he might have missed that blessing.

Jesus taught His disciples that when they showed hospitality to others, they were effectively showing it to Him (see Matthew 25:34–40). Peter further instructed, "Be hospitable to one another without grumbling" (1 Peter 4:9). The Shunammite woman provided hospitality without begrudging the cost, and the Lord used this warmth to bless and strengthen His servant Elisha. He also blessed the Shunammite couple, giving them a son in their old age and then miraculously raising him from the dead. Hospitality is a gift that blesses twice, giving to the giver as well as the receiver.

God is in control of life and death. Elisha faced the timeless dilemma: what to get the woman who had everything. Unlike the widow who was on the verge of starvation, the Shunammite woman had wealth and a husband. However, she was also barren, and it seems that she had given up hope of ever having a child. Elisha knew that only God could give life, and thus if she received a baby it would be obvious that it was a gift from the Lord.

But when the child later died, the Shunammite woman knew that this, too, was from the Lord. She did not blame her husband, sickness, or any other factor for the boy's death but instead went straight to the man of God. Likewise, Elisha knew the child's death was from the Lord. In fact, it was obvious that no power inherent in Elisha raised the boy to life; rather, it was God who answered Elisha's fervent prayer. Just as the boy's death was from the Lord, so too was his new life.

Many centuries earlier, a man named Job had lost his children to untimely deaths. When his family was killed by demonically inspired but divinely permitted marauders, Job declared, "The LORD gave, and the LORD has taken away" (Job 1:21). Later he asked his wife, "Shall we indeed accept good from God, and shall we not also accept adversity?" (Job 2:10). Job understood that all life is under the control of God. For this reason, we can have confidence in the face of death, but we can also rejoice that our God is the author of life.

REFLECTING ON THE TEXT

5) Why do we tend to see and appreciate God's grace the most when we are the most in need? How is this true in both the physical and spiritual realms?

_____

_____

_____

6) In Luke 7:47, Jesus said that the person who is forgiven much loves much, while the person who is forgiven little loves little. What do you think Jesus meant? How do you see that principle at work with both the widow and the Shunammite woman?

_____

_____

_____

_____

7) Consider some people in your life who have been hospitable to you. What did they do that was helpful? What did it cost them? How were you blessed?

_____

_____

_____

_____

8) Are there any situations in your life that seem out of control at present? If so, how can you rest in faith that God is in control? How does the knowledge that God is in control help you trust in Him?

_____

_____

_____

_____

PERSONAL RESPONSE

9) Are you thankful for the daily provisions God gives to you right now, or have you started to take these blessings for granted? How can you learn to be more dependent on God for the basics in your life?

_____

_____

_____

_____

10) Spend some time making a list of things for which you are thankful. Then spend time each day this week thanking God for these things. Add items to the list as He brings them to mind, and ask Him to teach you contentment.

_____

_____

_____

_____

4

NAAMAN AND GEHAZI
2 Kings 5:1–27

DRAWING NEAR

What are some expectations that people have of God and some "rules" that they expect Him to follow? What happens when God doesn't react in the way people anticipate He will?

_____

_____

_____

THE CONTEXT

In a previous study, we saw how the Lord gave Jehoshaphat and the people of Judah a miraculous victory over their enemies, the Ammonites, Moabites, and people of Mount Seir (see 2 Chronicles 20). In this study, we will discover that the Lord also gave victories to the enemies of Israel and Judah—even victories against His own people. At first glance, this seems shocking, because it might not fit our own preconceived expectations of how God works. But it is important to recognize that the Lord's plans often contradict our expectations. He works in and through the lives of all people, even nonbelievers, to accomplish His sovereign plans.

This issue of what people expect God to do as compared to what God is actually doing is an issue that surfaces repeatedly in 2 Kings 5. We will meet a man named Naaman, a great general and powerful friend of the king of Syria, who also happened to have leprosy, which was a disfiguring disease that one would expect would disqualify him from such high-profile service. We will also meet a lowly slave girl—a powerless young person who was taken from Israel and forced to live in a land of pagans. One might expect such a girl to wilt and dry up spiritually under such circumstances, but instead we will find the opposite to be true.

In contrast to this little slave girl, we will also see more of the character of Gehazi, Elisha's right-hand man whom he was grooming to take up the prophet's mantle of leadership. We would expect such a man to act with wisdom and propriety, but unfortunately that expectation will also prove wrong. This theme of human expectation and the sovereignty of God runs strong through this study, and the people we will meet will demonstrate how such expectations can be dangerous. Ironically, it will be a Gentile general who will teach an Israelite the proper way to obey God, even when His commands are surprising.

KEYS TO THE TEXT

Read 2 Kings 5:1–27, noting the key words and phrases indicated below.

> NAAMAN THE SYRIAN: *Naaman is a great man in Syria who is powerful, respected—and a leper.*

5:1. NAAMAN, COMMANDER OF THE ARMY: His name means "gracious." Nothing is known of Naaman outside of this chapter, but what we are told here is quite striking. The description of him as "great and honorable" indicates that he was probably renowned and powerful, and he maintained a reputation as being a man of good character.

BY HIM THE LORD HAD GIVEN VICTORY TO SYRIA: This statement reminds us that all victories come from God, and He can give those victories to anyone, regardless of whether or not they fear Him. In addition, there is a possibility that some of Naaman's military victories were against Israel, which seems paradoxical. Why would the Lord grant a victory to His people's enemies, especially if that victory meant His people's defeat? Yet we must remember that Israel at this time was apostate—chasing after pagan gods and spurning the ways of the true God—and He was using the Syrians to urge them to return to Him. At the same time, He also blessed Naaman by bringing him into the knowledge of Himself.

A LEPER: Despite his great stature, Naaman suffered from leprosy. Lepers were generally treated as outcasts in Old Testament times. It is a further proof of Naaman's great stature in Syria that his condition did not interfere with his high position at the king's court.

2. BROUGHT BACK CAPTIVE A YOUNG GIRL: From the vantage point of the young girl, being enslaved and led away to a foreign land was undoubtedly a terrible fate. Yet, contrary to expectation, the Lord had greater plans in mind for her. From an eternal perspective, her temporary suffering would become worthwhile, as the Lord used her to lead Naaman to a knowledge of Himself. The Lord would use Daniel in a similar way when he was later taken into captivity just prior to the exile of God's people.

3. HE WOULD HEAL HIM OF HIS LEPROSY: This unnamed girl evidently remained faithful to God in spite of her difficult circumstances. She was alone in a foreign land, and far removed from anyone who worshiped the Lord, but still she demonstrated a strong faith in God's healing power. She knew that God would heal her master if only Naaman would ask God's prophet Elisha—even though Naaman was a Gentile and an enemy of Israel.

4. THUS AND THUS SAID THE GIRL: Naaman may well have been desperate to find a cure for his leprosy and willing even to follow the advice of a lowly slave girl. Whatever his motivation, listening to her advice was his first step of faith. This also demonstrates how the Lord uses the faithful testimonies of His people, even from those the world deems insignificant.

SEEKING OUT ELISHA: Naaman heads to Israel in search of Elisha, the famous prophet, carrying a letter with him from the powerful king of Syria.

5. TEN TALENTS OF SILVER: Naaman's gift was literally fit for a king. It consisted of approximately 750 pounds of silver, 150 pounds of gold, and ten complete outfits of kingly raiment. The gold alone was equivalent to the annual wages of more than 500 common laborers.

7. AM I GOD: One can hardly blame King Joram for his response to the letter from the king of Syria. Note that the letter said Naaman had arrived before Joram "that you may heal him of his leprosy," as though the Syrians expected Joram to perform the miracle. It was not far-fetched for Joram to think the Syrians were inventing some impossible task in order to have an excuse for open war. Nevertheless, Joram's response also betrayed a lack of faith in God's willingness to answer prayer. He correctly noted that only God can "kill and make alive," but he showed no inclination to ask God for Naaman's healing.

8. HE SHALL KNOW THAT THERE IS A PROPHET IN ISRAEL: Elisha recognized the golden opportunity the king had missed: the chance to show the surrounding nations that the God of Israel was the one true God. Even from a political perspective, healing a Syrian could only be good for relations between Syria and Israel. But from an eternal perspective, Elisha knew this opportunity might well bring a soul into relationship with God. Elisha well understood that one soul is worth more than all the gold in the world.

9. HE STOOD AT THE DOOR OF ELISHA'S HOUSE: Naaman's failing appears to have been his vanity. He was accustomed to being treated with great deference, and in this situation he probably felt that the prophet was his social inferior.

10. ELISHA SENT A MESSENGER: This messenger was probably Gehazi, Elisha's servant. Previously, he had also used him as an intermediary with the woman from Shunem (see 2 Kings 4). It again appears this was Elisha's way of mentoring Gehazi, as Elijah had mentored him.

ELISHA'S PRESCRIPTION: Elisha tells Naaman to dip himself seven times in the Jordan River. This is not what the great commander of Syria expected.

10. WASH IN THE JORDAN SEVEN TIMES: Elisha's instructions were designed to demonstrate clearly to Naaman that his healing was from God alone, not from some mystical power.

11. NAAMAN BECAME FURIOUS: Naaman's anger had several causes. First, he had been treated (as he saw it) with contempt by a social inferior, as the prophet would not even trouble himself to come out and speak with him—and this after being received properly at the court of Israel's king. Second,

he probably thought Elisha was instructing him on how to become ritually cleansed without actually healing the leprosy. Bathing was an integral part of ritual cleansing, both in Israel and in the pagan nations, but Naaman wanted to be healed of his physical ailment, not of his spiritual condition. Elisha, however, was seeking to accomplish both.

WAVE HIS HAND: Naaman's expectations were somewhat amusing, and they also indicated his pagan background. He evidently expected Elisha to come forth, wave his hand over the leprosy, and he would be healed. He still had no knowledge of the omnipotent God of creation.

13. MY FATHER: It was not normal for servants to address their master in this way; rather, it was more fitting in a mentoring relationship (such as Elisha had with Elijah). This indicates once again the character of Naaman, for even his servants viewed him as a father figure. Indeed, their intercession here indicated they sincerely wanted to see him healed.

IF THE PROPHET HAD TOLD YOU TO DO SOMETHING GREAT: The servants demonstrated keen insight and wisdom in giving this advice. Naaman was clearly prepared to do anything in order to be healed of his leprosy, and it was all the better that the required action was so easy. Yet this principle also applies on a larger scale to our fallen human nature, which often leads us to think we can atone for our sins by performing some spiritual feat or costly penance. The true means of salvation is found in confessing our sins, asking forgiveness, and trusting in Christ's sacrifice. It is the very simplicity of this message that often causes sinners to reject God's offer.

A SOUL IS SAVED: Naaman sees that the Lord is the one true God and believes with all his heart.

15. NOW I KNOW THAT THERE IS NO GOD IN ALL THE EARTH, EXCEPT IN ISRAEL: Naaman went to Israel to find healing for his physical disease but left both physically *and* spiritually healed. His statement is a clear declaration of faith in God. It also puts to shame a great portion of Israel, the very people who were supposed to be a testimony to the world around them of the power and presence of the one true God. Instead, they tried to worship both God and Baal.

16. I WILL RECEIVE NOTHING: Elisha rejected Naaman's gift because he wanted it to be absolutely clear that he was in no way responsible for Naaman's

healing. Elisha did accept gifts at other times, including the hospitality of the woman from Shunem, but such gifts were intended to support the ministry of a man of God. Naaman's gift was intended as payment for services rendered, and God's people are never to seek profit from God's grace. As we shall see, Gehazi did not understand this principle.

18. MAY THE LORD PARDON YOUR SERVANT: Naaman also anticipated difficulty when he returned home to Syria, as he apparently was required in his job to accompany the king to pagan worship ceremonies. He did not yet understand that the God who healed his incurable disease could also resolve his difficult circumstances.

19. GO IN PEACE: Elisha's response to Naaman demonstrates God's patience and mercy. The Lord wants His people to grow in their knowledge of His character and His Word, but He is not a harsh taskmaster. The Lord does not demand that a new convert grow into spiritual maturity overnight.

GEHAZI'S GREED: *Elisha's servant is overwhelmed with the greatness of Naaman's gift and yields to deadly temptation.*

20. MY MASTER HAS SPARED NAAMAN THIS SYRIAN: Elisha's servant, Gehazi, revealed some degree of resentment and national prejudice in these words. He seemed to resent Naaman's healing, preferring to see him perish, but his hostility clouded his thinking. He should have rejoiced in Naaman's conversion rather than wishing him ill simply because he was "this Syrian."

22. MY MASTER HAS SENT ME: One sin leads to another, and in this case Gehazi's covetousness led to telling lies. Yet Gehazi's lie was even more insidious because it impugned not only Elisha's character but God's as well. Naaman was a new believer, and his understanding of God's ways was incomplete—and here was the servant of God's spokesman saying that God's prophets did, in fact, accept payment for their services. Gehazi was not only grasping profit for himself but also stealing from God's glory.

23. TWO TALENTS OF SILVER: This is approximately 150 pounds of silver. It was more than five years' salary for the common laborer in the economy of that time.

THEY CARRIED THEM ON AHEAD OF HIM: It would have been difficult for Gehazi to carry 150 pounds of silver by himself, but having a servant run ahead indicated that a man was important in some way. Gehazi was indulging his desire for recognition and human praise as well as for wealth. Both are simply forms of covetousness, and both can still be snares for Christians today.

24. STORED THEM AWAY IN THE HOUSE: Gehazi's sin is reminiscent of the sin of Achan, who tried to hide stolen loot by burying it under his tent—which cost the lives of Achan and his whole family (see Joshua 7).

25. YOUR SERVANT DID NOT GO ANYWHERE: Gehazi also lied to Elisha, adding another sin to the list.

26. DID NOT MY HEART GO WITH YOU: The Lord had revealed Gehazi's actions to Elisha, and the prophet knew the truth even before he asked Gehazi where he had gone. In fact, by asking that question, Elisha was offering Gehazi a chance to confess his sin and repent. His use of the word *heart* rather than *mind* suggests the affection he had for his servant. Elisha probably had great hopes that Gehazi would take up his mantle one day, just as he had done for Elijah. But on this sad day those hopes died.

27. THE LEPROSY OF NAAMAN SHALL CLING TO YOU: Gehazi's act betrayed a lack of faith in the Lord's ability to provide. As a result, Elisha condemned Gehazi and his descendants to suffer Naaman's skin disease forever. The punishment was a twist for Gehazi, who had gone to take something from Naaman, but what he received was Naaman's disease.

UNLEASHING THE TEXT

1) Why did Elisha instruct Naaman to wash seven times in the Jordan River? What would have happened if he had refused to do so? What did he gain by obeying?

_____

_____

_____

_____

2) What motivated Gehazi to take the gift from Naaman? Why did this action bring leprosy on him? What harm did his actions cause to others beside himself?

_____

_____

_____

_____

3) How did Naaman's character compare with Gehazi's? What were the priorities in each man's life? How did each respond to God's commands?

_____

_____

_____

_____

4) How did Gehazi's attitude toward Naaman compare with that of Naaman's slave girl? How did each of them view the unbelieving Gentiles?

_____

_____

_____

_____

EXPLORING THE MEANING

God pours out His blessings on those who believe in Him. The Syrians were not members of God's chosen people, the descendants of Abraham. What's worse, they were Israel's enemy, engaged in long-standing border raids, and frequently carried Israelites away into slavery. Naaman himself was a powerful general, and he probably was responsible (from a human standpoint) for Syria's victories over the Lord's people. Yet when he asked God's prophet for healing of an incurable disease, the Lord honored his faith and his request.

The reason for God's grace in healing Naaman was that the Lord is eager to pour out His blessings on those who exercise faith in Him, regardless of that person's background or upbringing. Indeed, the Lord had been the one who gave Naaman his great victories and successes—even against His own people. The Lord did this to bless Naaman and move him toward a faith in Himself, but He also gave Naaman success in order to move the people of Israel back into obedience to His Word. The sad truth is that the Lord wanted to pour out His blessings on Israel as well, but His people refused to ask. A Gentile had exercised more faith than the people of God were willing to show.

Jesus addressed this issue when He spoke of the fact that a prophet is not honored among his own people. He told His listeners there were many widows in Israel during the great famine of Elijah's time, but God's prophet went to none of them—instead, he went to a Gentile widow. There were also many lepers in Israel during Elisha's time, but God's prophet healed none of them—only Naaman the Syrian (see Luke 4:24–27). God wanted to help them all, but the Gentiles were the only ones who asked for His help. Today, as then, the Lord wants to help one and all—but He does require that we trust Him.

The Lord calls us to obey Him, even if His commands don't meet our expectations. Naaman was a great and powerful leader in one of the world's mightiest nations, and he was accustomed to being treated with deference. He was a general in the army, and his soldiers saluted him and obeyed his orders. He was a wealthy and influential man in the king's court, and his peers addressed him with respect. But when he arrived at the door of a lowly prophet, a foreign seer who had no wealth or pomp, he found himself standing outside and being addressed by the prophet's servant. This was not what he expected.

Naaman had traveled to Israel to find a man of great power who could heal him of his incurable leprosy. Elisha did not act as Naaman expected. Instead, he told Naaman to go away and bathe in a muddy river, which indicated the prophet was not even the one who would heal him. The entire experience was quite shocking to Naaman, because nothing fit his expectations. Nevertheless, Naaman eventually obeyed the command of God, and his skin was miraculously healed. More important, his soul was saved and his spiritual eyes were opened to an understanding of the God of Israel.

Naaman had to let go of his own expectations and desires and submit himself to obey God's commands, given through His prophet, even though they didn't make any sense to him at the time. God's ways are not our ways, and we cannot comprehend all of God's sovereign purposes and designs. There are times when He commands us to do things that are contrary to our culture's teachings, to what everyone else is doing, and to everything that we would expect. At such times, we must remember that God's ways are always right, regardless of what the world may tell us, and we can only follow Him by obeying His ways.

The sin of covetousness can destroy a person's ministry. Gehazi was privileged to work beside Elisha and had a unique ministry. He assisted the prophet in performing great miracles, and he was blessed with hearing the Word of God, day in and day out, right from the mouth of God's chief spokesman in Israel. He probably also had a great ministry ahead of him, as Elisha was evidently training him to take on the mantle of prophetic leadership when the time came. These things indicate he was a godly man who was qualified for such a ministry as few others would have been. He undoubtedly had some rough edges, as we all do, but the Lord was at work to smooth out those rough spots and equip him for greater areas of service.

But Gehazi was dazzled by the immense wealth of Naaman's gift—enough gold and silver for him to live in comfort for the rest of his days. He also coveted honor and prestige, as he walked behind two servants who carried his newfound loot like a triumphant warrior returning from battle. Perhaps Gehazi justified such indulgences by telling himself how he would use the wealth and honor to further the Lord's work. But even such excuses do not justify greed. The truth is that he had "cashed in" on God's grace, using God's work of salvation for his own material gain—and this sin resulted in permanent damage to his ministry.

Gehazi's sin did not end his walk with God, for he appeared later still serving Elisha. However, it did damage his testimony and severely hinder his future effectiveness in ministry. This principle holds true for any area of sin. The Lord does not abandon His children when they indulge in sinful behavior, but such disobedience may permanently disqualify us from future areas of service. The Bible instructs us on how to avoid the tragedy of Gehazi: "Do not love the world or the things in the world. If anyone loves the world, the love of the Father is not in him. For all that is in the world—the lust of the flesh, the lust of the eyes, and the pride of life—is not of the Father but is of the world" (1 John 2:15–16).

Reflecting on the Text

5) Why did God choose to heal Naaman, even though he was an unbeliever and a Gentile? Why did God give him military victories over His own people?

_____

_____

_____

6) In what ways were both Naaman and Gehazi shocked by Elisha's words? How did each man respond to God's unexpected instructions? How did the actions of an unsaved Gentile add shame to one of God's people?

_____

_____

_____

7) In your own words, define the following sins and provide examples of each.

Lust of the flesh:

_____

_____

_____

Lust of the eyes:

_____

_____

_____

_____

_____

Pride of life:

_____

_____

_____

_____

8) When has God's Word called you to do something that surprised you? How did His commands contradict your expectations? How did you respond?

_____

_____

_____

_____

_____

PERSONAL RESPONSE

9) Are you struggling with some sin that might threaten your testimony for the Lord? If so, how will you follow the example of Naaman rather than Gehazi?

_____

_____

_____

_____

10) How do you tend to treat non-Christians? How can you direct them toward faith in Christ?

_____

_____

_____

5

THE SIEGE OF SAMARIA

2 Kings 6:8–7:20

DRAWING NEAR

What are some ways in which God works "behind the scenes" in our world? What glimpses does He give us to reveal His power, authority, and sovereign control over His creation?

_____

_____

_____

THE CONTEXT

The healing of Naaman reveals that the Lord often surprises us with the way in which He accomplishes His plans. He works in and through the lives of people from all walks of life, faith, and belief, using them to sovereignly chore-ograph and fulfill His greater purposes on earth. In this study, we also see God at work—through Elisha, through supernatural phenomena, and through the people in and around the northern kingdom of Israel.

As we open this study, the kingdom of Israel was under the rule of Joram, the younger son of Ahab. Like the rest of his family, Joram was not a godly king but seems to have been divided in his loyalties. He relied on God's words through the prophet Elisha when it benefited him, but he blamed Elisha and God when his nation experienced suffering. Ultimately, he failed to recognize that his sin was at the heart of his difficulties.

God wanted the people of Israel to recognize that He was sovereignly able to control events in order accomplish his purposes. To demonstrate this fact, He leaked the king of Syria's plans to Elisha, who in turn reported all that He heard God say to Joram. This frustrated the Syrian king to no end, so he sent an army to subdue the prophet. The Syrian army surrounded the town where Elisha was staying, bringing his servant to despair. But Elisha told him not to fear, for he could see something with his "spiritual eyes" that the servant could not.

As we will discover, the same is true for us today. God is always surrounding us with His armies—and He is always orchestrating events according to His purposes, not our own.

Keys to the Text

Read 2 Kings 6:8–7:20, noting the key words and phrases indicated below.

> The Syrians' Secrets: *The king of Syria makes plans to attack Israel, but somehow his secrets keep making their way to the king of Israel.*

8. king of Syria: This was likely Ben-Hadad II. The Syrian king was probably sending raiding parties to pillage and plunder Israelite towns.

9. the man of God: The Lord gave Elisha miraculous revelations concerning the Syrians' military plans, even though he was living in Israel, far to the south.

10. not just once or twice: Elisha continually identified to King Joram the Israelite towns the king of Syria planned to attack. Joram then took the proper precautions and appropriately fortified those towns in order to frustrate the Syrian plans.

11. which of us is for the king of Israel: The king of Syria was mystified as to how Joram could continue to anticipate his plans of attack. The only sensible answer, from a human perspective, was that he had a spy in his court.

12. ELISHA, THE PROPHET WHO IS IN ISRAEL: It is significant that Elisha's fame had spread into the Syrians' own court. Undoubtedly, word had spread of the miracles the Lord worked through him, yet it is also true the world takes note of those who stand faithfully for the Lord.

13. HE IS IN DOTHAN: A town in the hill country of Manasseh, located about ten miles north of Samaria and twelve miles south of Jezreel. Dothan commanded a key mountain pass along a main road that connected Damascus and Egypt.

14. A GREAT ARMY: The king of Syria sent a sizable force, including horses and chariots, to take Elisha prisoner. The army encircled the town of Dothan.

15. WHAT SHALL WE DO: The servant's consternation was quite understandable. Imagine his shock and dismay to step outside and discover that an enemy army had swept in silently during the night to surround his city in great force. But the servant did the right thing: he turned to the man of God for guidance.

16. DO NOT FEAR: Once again, we are reminded that fear is the enemy of God's people. The servant's initial response was a reflexive fear, but Elisha commanded him to put away that fear and rely instead on the power of God. Fear can cause a Christian to take rash and unwise actions, but turning the problem over to God in prayer will overcome the terror.

THOSE WHO ARE WITH US: Picture Elisha's servant looking around him with a puzzled expression at these words, wondering to whom the prophet was referring. Elisha, in fact, was not referring to any earthly power at all but to the heavenly hosts whom the servant's fleshly eyes could not see.

SPIRITUAL SIGHT, PHYSICAL BLINDNESS: The Lord allows the servant of Elisha to see His spiritual reality and blinds the Syrians to the physical realm.

17. OPEN HIS EYES THAT HE MAY SEE: Elisha asked the Lord to enable His servant's physical eyes to see the hidden spiritual world for a moment so that his faith might be strengthened. This is the essence of faith: to believe firmly in that which one cannot see and simply rely on God's promises (see Hebrews 11:1).

18. HE STRUCK THEM WITH BLINDNESS: The Lord had opened the servant's eyes to see the spiritual reality around him, and now He closed the

Syrians' eyes so they could not even see the physical world. Those who lack spiritual sight are no better than these Syrian soldiers, stumbling through life like blind men. Spiritual sight, however, can only come from faith in Jesus Christ.

19. Follow me . . . to the man whom you seek: By going to Samaria himself, Elisha did not lie but led the Syrian army to where he ultimately would be found.

21. Shall I kill them . . . shall I kill them: King Joram's eagerness is almost amusing. He would certainly have been within his rights from a military point of view to slaughter the soldiers, since they had invaded Israel in force. But the Lord intended to demonstrate His mercy and grace, even to the enemies of His people.

22. Set food and water before them: The act of sparing the soldiers' lives demonstrated mercy, withholding the death or captivity that was due them as a defeated army. But the Lord had His people go beyond mercy, providing a great banquet for their enemies and sending them back home in peace—and this demonstrated His grace.

22. You shall not kill them: Elisha, bearing divinely delegated authority, prohibited the execution of the captives. This kindness would testify to the goodness of God and likely stall future opposition from the Syrian raiders. These kind deeds gained a moral conquest.

23. A great feast: In the ancient Near East, a common meal could signify the making of a covenant between two parties (see Leviticus 7:15–18).

The Famine: The Syrian king is not pleased that his strategies for conquering Israel have not gone according to plan, so he summons his entire army for a massive siege against Samaria.

24. Ben-Hadad . . . gathered all his army: In contrast to the smaller raiding parties and the larger force seeking Elisha's capture, Ben-Hadad II gathered his *entire* army and marched to Samaria.

25. Donkey's head was sold for eighty shekels of silver: The siege resulted in a terrible famine gripping the city of Samaria. A donkey's head—an ignominious body part of an unclean animal—sold at an overvalued price of about two pounds of silver.

Dove droppings for five shekels of silver: "Dove droppings" was either a nickname for some small pea or root or literal dung to be used as fuel or food in the desperate situation. Approximately one pint cost about two ounces of silver.

26. HELP, MY LORD, O KING: The woman asked King Joram to render a legal decision in her dispute with another woman.

28. GIVE YOUR SON, THAT WE MAY EAT HIM: The curses of the Mosaic covenant, especially for the sin of apostasy, predicted this sort of pagan cannibalism (see Deuteronomy 28:52–57). The way in which the woman presented her case without feeling added to the horror of the proceedings.

30. TORE HIS CLOTHES: Joram tore his clothes as a sign of distress and grief. He also put "sackcloth" on his body—a coarse cloth made from goat's hair—as a sign of mourning. However, in spite of these outward expressions, he was not truly humbled for his and the nation's sin, or he would not have called for vengeance on Elisha.

MURDEROUS RAGE: *King Joram is stunned by the famine in Samaria and vows to take revenge on Elisha, whom he wrongly assumes is behind all their suffering.*

31. THE HEAD OF ELISHA: It is possible Joram issued this death sentence against Elisha because he viewed the siege as the work of the Lord, and thus assumed the Lord's representative—the prophet with whom the kings of Israel were in conflict—was involved as well. It is also possible he thought Elisha's clemency to the Syrian army had somehow led to and added intensity to the present siege, or that he was angry that Elisha had not ended the famine through his "miracle power." However, most likely the reason he wanted Elisha dead was because he expected his own mourning would have resulted in the end of the siege. When it did not, he sought the prophet's head.

32. THE ELDERS WERE SITTING WITH HIM: The elders were the leading citizens of Samaria, so this gathering indicated the high regard in which the prominent people of Samarian society held Elisha. The prophet said that the "son of a murderer" had sent someone to kill him, which could both mean that Joram was the son of Ahab, who was guilty of murder (see 1 Kings 21:1–16), or that he just had the character of a murderer.

33. WHY SHOULD I WAIT FOR THE LORD ANY LONGER: Joram viewed God as the instigator of the siege and famine in Samaria, and he saw no hope the Lord would reverse the situation.

THE SYRIANS FLEE: Elisha prophesies the famine will come to an end by the next day, and the Lord miraculously delivers the people of Israel from the Syrian army.

7:1. A SEAH . . . FOR A SHEKEL: Elisha said that about seven quarts of flour would sell for about two-fifths of an ounce of silver, and about thirteen or fourteen quarts of barley would sell for about two-fifths of an ounce of silver. These prices, when compared to those in 2 Kings 6:25, indicated that the next day the famine in Samaria would end.

AT THE GATE: In ancient Israel, the city gate was the marketplace where business was transacted. Normal trade at the city gate of Samaria implied that the siege would be lifted.

2. AN OFFICER ON WHOSE HAND THE KING LEANED: This royal official questioned the Lord's ability to provide food within the day. For that offense, Elisha predicted the officer would witness the promised miracle but would not partake in any of it.

3. FOUR LEPROUS MEN: The author of Kings uses the account of these lepers to tell of the siege's end and the provisions for Samaria. These lepers lived in the area immediately outside the city gate, where they had been shut out of Samaria due to their disease. The lepers knew that living in Samaria, whether just outside or inside the gate, offered them nothing but death.

5. THE OUTSKIRTS OF THE SYRIAN CAMP: The normal meaning of this phrase would refer to the back edge of the army camp—the farthest point from the wall of Samaria.

6. THE HITTITES AND . . . THE EGYPTIANS: The Lord had made the Syrians hear the sound of a huge army approaching, and they thought the Israelite king had hired the armies of the Hittites and the Egyptians to attack them. The Hittites were descendants of the once great Hittite empire and lived in small groups across northern Syria. Egypt was in decline at this time, but its army still represented a great danger to the Syrians.

THE SYRIANS FLEE: The four lepers decide they must share the good news of their deliverance with King Joram, but their story is met with skepticism.

9. PUNISHMENT WILL COME UPON US: The lepers did not fear that the Syrians would return but that the Lord would punish them for their sin of not telling King Joram of their discovery.

12. WHAT THE SYRIANS HAVE DONE TO US: Joram greeted the report from the lepers with great suspicion. He thought the Syrians were feigning the pullback to appear defeated. They would then lure the Israelites out of Samaria for a surprise attack to gain entrance into the city.

15. SO THE MESSENGERS RETURNED: The king of Israel sent out a small party consisting of two chariots to investigate the lepers' report. When the party found the road strewn with the weapons and garments the Syrian army had thrown away in their panic, they knew for sure that the threat to the city of Samaria had ended.

18. SO IT HAPPENED JUST AS THE MAN OF GOD HAD SPOKEN: By repeating words from verses 1 and 2 and by explicit statements ("according to the word of the LORD" and "just as the man of God had spoken), the text emphasizes that Elisha's prophecy had literally come to pass.

UNLEASHING THE TEXT

1) Elisha was often referred to as "the man of God" (2 Kings 6:6). What does this tell you about his relationship with God? What does it tell you about his reputation in Israel?

2) How did Elisha respond to the presence of the Syrian armies around the city of Dothan? How did his servant respond? What does this tell us about the strength of God?

3) How did Joram feel toward God in regard to the famine and siege of Samaria? Why did he want Elisha killed? What does this say about his understanding of the situation?

_____

_____

_____

4) What did the lepers do when they discovered the Syrians had left? What motivated them to share the news with the city? Considering all the times Joram had seen God's hand at work, what does his response tell you about the state of his heart?

_____

_____

_____

EXPLORING THE MEANING

God is sensitive to the needs of His people. As those who are faithful to God seek His help, they are rewarded with glimpses of His miraculous hand at work. When Elisha's servant saw the armies of Syria around the city of Dothan, he was struck with fear and cried out, "What shall we do?" (2 Kings 6:15). In response, God allowed the servant to see behind the scenes into the spiritual realm, and he was comforted by the angelic hosts he saw surrounding the city.

Our God has a great plan for the nations, but he also turns His attention to the small, to the insignificant in the world's eyes, to the individual. We can look at a beautiful sunset and see the majesty of God at work, or experience the incredible shock of an earthquake, or witness the demise of an evil empire, and recognize in all these things that God is sovereign. Yet God's sovereignty also extends to the small details of our lives. He cared about the servant's fear, which is why He instructed Elisha to say to him, "Do not fear, for those who are with us are more than those who are with them" (verse 16).

Jesus would later reiterate that God is concerned with the smaller details of life by supernaturally providing money for the disciples' temple tax. Jesus, the Son of God, was not under the priests' authority, yet He chose to pay the tax so as not to offend them. He said to Peter, "Nevertheless, lest we offend them, go to the sea, cast in a hook, and take the fish that comes up first. And when you have opened its mouth, you will find a piece of money; take that and give it to them for Me and you" (Matthew 17:27). God sovereignly provided for Peter's need, but He also used the event to encourage his faith in God's love and care.

God demonstrates both mercy and grace through Christ. Elisha delivered the Syrian army into the hands of King Joram by walking them right into the middle of his fortified capital city. This army had come in force against Israel and had intended to fully overrun them once they had captured the prophet of God. For this reason, King Joram would have been justified in taking the men as slaves or putting them to death. No sensible king in that situation would have set the army free, allowing the Syrians to regroup and return in greater force at a later date.

Yet this is exactly what the Lord commanded Joram to do: set the enemies free and allow them to return to Syria in peace. This was God's demonstration to the Syrians that He was a merciful and forgiving God. This deed would have been remarkable enough by itself, but God's generosity did not stop there. He further commanded Joram to give the enemy army a great banquet and treat them as honored guests rather than captured and hostile soldiers. This was the grace of God in action.

Mercy is the withholding of judgment that is rightfully due, but grace goes one step further by providing gifts to those who deserve death. Both of these qualities are found in perfect fullness in Jesus Christ. All humankind deserves God's wrath and judgment, "for the wages of sin is death" (Romans 6:23), but God in His mercy grants full forgiveness by imputing our sins to His Son. God then goes beyond this gift by pouring out His blessings on us, even to the point of giving us the presence of His Holy Spirit. Truly, as Paul wrote, our God "is able to do exceedingly abundantly above all that we ask or think, according to the power that works in us" (Ephesians 3:20), and we enjoy all these blessings through His Son, Jesus Christ.

Our security does not lie in military might. The Syrians boasted a powerful military in Elisha's day. Israel's army was also significant, yet the Syrians did not hesitate to send a powerful force deep into Israel's heart, nearly to the gates of her capital city. Their chariots and trained soldiers surrounded Samaria, cutting off food and supplies to the city, and the people of Samaria endured a great famine. Who could save them from such an overwhelming foe that had come on them with such breathtaking suddenness and ferocity?

Elisha knew the answer to that question, and he was not the least bit troubled by the situation. He knew the hope of God's people is His character, not any military weapon or scheme of man. Even when King Joram blamed him for the tragedy and sought his head, Elisha did not waver, for he knew that he operated in the power of God. By the end of the next day, the army of Syria had fled in fear, leaving their garments and weapons behind. Both Israel and Syria learned a nation's security lies in God's power, not its own military might.

This principle is as true today as it was in Elisha's generation, for God is just as faithful to deliver His people now as He was in Old Testament times. God calls His people to place their faith completely in Him, not in any form of human government or military. Isaiah warned, "Woe to those who go down to Egypt for help, and rely on horses, who trust in chariots because they are many, and in horsemen because they are very strong, but who do not look to the Holy One of Israel, nor seek the LORD!" (Isaiah 31:1). We need to emulate Elisha by asking the Lord to open our spiritual eyes so we can see His mighty hand and be encouraged.

REFLECTING ON THE TEXT

5) Why did God tell Elisha the secret plans of the Syrian king? What does this teach about His character? What does it teach about the way He protects His people?

_____

_____

_____

6) Why did God command King Joram to feed the Syrian army and send them home? How did this affect the Israelites? How did it affect the Syrians?

_____

_____

_____

_____

7) Israel's king wanted to strike down the Syrian army. Would he have been justified in doing so? What do you learn about God's character toward His enemies from this account?

_____

_____

_____

_____

8) Why did God allow the Syrians to besiege Samaria? Why did He allow the famine to occur? What was He revealing to the people by delivering them in the way He did?

_____

_____

_____

_____

_____

PERSONAL RESPONSE

9) How has your understanding of God's power been impacted by your study of His Word? How can you pray for "spiritual sight" to see God's hand at work around you?

_____

_____

_____

_____

10) How does the Lord command us to demonstrate both mercy and grace to others? To whom might He be calling you to show His grace this week?

_____

_____

_____

_____

6

THE END OF AHAB'S LINE
2 Kings 9:1–10:36

DRAWING NEAR

What happens when people ignore the warnings that a severe thunderstorm, tornado, or hurricane is heading their way? What is the natural result of making such a decision?

THE CONTEXT

God had miraculously intervened to save the kingdom of Israel from a siege by the Syrian army. Following this battle, King Ben-Hadad II of Syria fell ill, and a servant named Hazael was sent to inquire of Elisha as to whether he would recover. Hazael was a commoner, but God had revealed to Elisha that he would take over the Syrian throne. God also revealed the atrocities Hazael would commit against God's people, which caused Elisha to weep (see 2 Kings 8:7–15).

God's Word came to pass. Hazael murdered Ben-Hadad II, became king of Syria, and went to war against Israel and Judah. By this time, the king of Judah was Ahaziah, the son of Jehoram of Judah. Ahaziah was an ungodly king, "for he was the son-in-law of the house of Ahab" (verse 27). (The fact Israel and Judah had two kings with the same names who ruled at around the same time makes it easy to confuse them.) Ahaziah and Joram collaborated against Hazael and attacked the Syrian army. The Bible doesn't tell us the outcome, but we do know that Joram was wounded and retreated to Jezreel (see verses 28–29).

At this point, the Lord intervened. He had previously told His prophet Elijah that a man named Jehu would rise up to become king over Israel, and that this man would put to death those involved in the worship of Baal (see 1 Kings 19:17). The time had come for this prophecy to be fulfilled, so Elisha covertly oversaw the anointing of this new king. As we will see in this study, while Jehu was not necessarily a man of God—and didn't always have the best of motives behind his actions—the Lord would nevertheless use him to fulfill His purposes.

KEYS TO THE TEXT

Read 2 Kings 9:1–10:36, noting the key words and phrases indicated below.

> JEHU BECOMES KING: *Elisha sends one of his student-prophets to secretly anoint Jehu, a commander of the forces of Israel, to be the next king in place of Joram.*

9:2. JEHU THE SON OF JEHOSHAPHAT: Elisha commissioned a prophet to anoint Jehu alone, behind closed doors, in a private room that could be closed off to the public. The rite was to be a secret affair without Elisha present so King Joram would not suspect a coup was coming.

3. ANOINTED YOU KING OVER ISRAEL: Anointing with olive oil indicated the Lord had chosen a person to be king (see 1 Samuel 10:1). In this way, the commissioned prophet was indicating to Jehu that God had invested him with the power to rule.

FLEE, AND DO NOT DELAY: Elisha underscored the danger of the assignment by telling the young prophet to flee after the anointing. The discovery of a prophet in the midst of Israel's camp would alert the pro-Joram elements to the possibility of the coup.

7. AVENGE THE BLOOD OF MY SERVANTS: Jehu was to be the Lord's avenger for the murders of His prophets (see 1 Kings 18:4) and of people such as Naboth who served Him (see 21:1–16).

9. LIKE THE HOUSE OF JEROBOAM . . . AND LIKE THE HOUSE OF BAASHA: God would thoroughly annihilate Ahab's line in the same way He had violently ended Jeroboam I's dynasty and Baasha's dynasty (see 1 Kings 15:27–30; 16:8–13).

PROPHECY AGAINST JEZEBEL: *The Lord tells Jehu what will become of Ahab's family, including his wife, the wicked Queen Jezebel.*

10. DOGS SHALL EAT JEZEBEL: The young prophet foretold that dogs, which were considered scavengers in the ancient Near East, would devour the corpse of Jezebel. This would take place on the plot of ground at Jezreel, which had formerly been the location of Naboth's vineyard.

NONE TO BURY HER: The Israelites buried their dead with the bones of ancestors in a common grave. The lack of such a burial was considered a severe punishment and disgrace.

11. THIS MADMAN: The soldier demonstrated his disdain for Elisha's servant by referring to him as crazy or demented. This same term was used in Jeremiah 29:26 and Hosea 9:7 as a derogatory reference for prophets whose messages were considered crazy. Jehu's response referred to the prophet's "babble," not his behavior.

12. THUS AND THUS HE SPOKE TO ME: Jehu repeated the prophecy to his troops that the commissioned prophet have given to him in verses 6–10.

13. THEY BLEW TRUMPETS: When the officers heard the prophecy, they laid their cloaks under Jehu's feet—with the steps of the house serving as a makeshift throne—and blew their trumpets to acclaim Jehu as king. A trumpet often heralded such a public proclamation and assembly, including the appointment of a king (see 1 Kings 1:34).

JORAM'S SURPRISE: *After Jehu is anointed as the next king of Israel, he pays a surprise visit to King Joram to forcibly take the throne from him.*

15. LET NO ONE LEAVE OR ESCAPE FROM THE CITY: King Joram was recuperating in the city of Jezreel after being wounded in the battle against Hazael of Syria. Jehu knew it was important to take Joram completely by surprise

if he wanted to succeed in his revolt and avoid a civil conflict. For this reason, he ordered the city of Ramoth Gilead, where he had been anointed, to be sealed lest someone loyal to Joram escape and notify the king.

16. WENT TO JEZREEL: From Ramoth Gilead, Jehu traveled due west in his chariot across the Jordan River, north of Mount Gilboa, to the town of Jezreel. Ahaziah, the king of Judah, was in town at the time to visit the recuperating Joram. It was an unfortunate bit of timing, as it placed him in the city during Jehu's purge.

21. NABOTH THE JEZREELITE: Providentially, the kings of Israel and Judah met Jehu at the very place where Ahab and Jezebel had put Naboth to death. Joram, by then aware of the impending disaster, summoned his forces and, accompanied by the king of Judah, met Jehu as his men ascended the slope up to the city from the northern side.

22. WHAT PEACE, AS LONG AS THE HARLOTRIES OF YOUR MOTHER: Joram was evidently still unsure of Jehu's rebellious plans and wished to know if his coming meant peace. Jehu replied there could be no true peace in Israel because of Jezebel's influence. *Harlotries*, a common biblical metaphor for idolatry and witchcraft (seeking information from demonic forces), described the nature of Jezebel's influence. Idolatry had lured Israel into demonic practices.

25. BIDKAR HIS CAPTAIN: The word *captain* originally referred to the third man in a chariot besides the driver and a warrior, whose task it was to hold the shield and arms of the warrior. The term was eventually applied to a high-ranking official. Jehu and Bidkar had either rode together in one chariot when Elijah gave his prediction of Ahab's death (see 1 Kings 21:17–24) or they were riding in different chariots behind Ahab.

THE LORD LAID THIS BURDEN UPON HIM: The term *burden* referred to a prophetic oracle; in this case, the prophetic utterance of Elijah as recorded in 1 Kings 21:20–24. Jehu viewed himself as God's avenging agent who would fulfill Elijah's prediction.

THE DEATH OF AHAZIAH: King Ahaziah of Judah flees for his life when he sees the arrow from Jehu strike King Joram in the heart. He meets the same unfortunate end.

27. AHAZIAH . . . FLED TO MEGIDDO, AND DIED THERE. Ahaziah fled by way of the road to Beth Haggan, a town seven miles southwest of Jezreel. Jehu and his men pursued Ahaziah and wounded him at the ascent of Gur by Ibleam, which

was just south of Beth Haggan. According to 2 Chronicles 22:9, Ahaziah reached Samaria, about eight miles south of Beth Haggan, where he hid for a while. Ahaziah then fled north to Megiddo, twelve miles north of Samaria, where he died.

29. TWELFTH YEAR: In 2 Kings 8:25, the author used the non-accession-year system of dating, so that Joram's accession year was counted as the first year of his reign. Here, the author used the accession-year dating system, where Joram's ascension year and his second year were counted as the first year of his reign.

JEZEBEL'S BITTER END: Jehu continues his duties in fulfilling the Lord's judgment on the house of Ahab by seeking the death of Jezebel. The former queen remains unrepentant to the end.

30. SHE PUT PAINT ON HER EYES: In ancient times, women painted their eyelids with a black powder mixed with oil and applied with a brush, which darkened them to give an enlarged effect. Jezebel's appearance at the window in Jezreel gave the air of a royal audience to awe Jehu. She probably recognized her end was upon her, yet she remained defiant and arrogant to the last.

31. ZIMRI, MURDERER OF YOUR MASTER: Zimri had overthrown King Elah and stolen the throne of Israel, but he had only sat on that throne for seven days (see 1 Kings 16:11–12). In referring to Jehu by this name, Jezebel was suggesting he had done the same thing and would meet the same end. She was wrong.

32. THREE EUNUCHS LOOKED OUT AT HIM: Some of Jezebel's own officials threw her out of a second-story window, after which Jehu drove his horses and chariots over her body.

34. SHE WAS A KING'S DAUGHTER: Jehu recognized Jezebel's royalty while denying that she deserved to be the queen of Israel.

36. THIS IS THE WORD OF THE LORD: The place and means in which Jezebel died thus fulfilled Elijah's prophetic oracle: "Concerning Jezebel the LORD also spoke, saying, 'The dogs shall eat Jezebel by the wall of Jezreel'" (1 Kings 21:23).

THE PURGE CONTINUES: Jehu's next move in securing the throne is to kill all of Ahab's male descendants. But Jehu then brings judgment on himself by executing Ahab's former officials.

10:1. AHAB HAD SEVENTY SONS: These were the male descendants of Ahab, both sons and grandsons. Ahab had a number of wives and, therefore, many descendants. These living relatives could avenge a dead kinsman by killing the person responsible for his death.

2. AS SOON AS THIS LETTER COMES TO YOU: Jehu sent the same message in a number of different letters to (1) the royal officials of Ahab's house, who had probably fled from the city of Jezreel (2) the leaders of the tribes of Israel (3) those who had been appointed as the custodians and educators of the royal children.

3. FIGHT FOR YOUR MASTER'S HOUSE: Jehu demanded that Ahab's appointed officials either fight to continue the royal line of Ahab or select a new king from Ahab's descendants to fight him in battle. This would decide which family would rule Israel.

5. IN CHARGE OF THE HOUSE . . . IN CHARGE OF THE CITY: These two officials were the palace administrator and the city governor (probably the commander of the city's fighting force). They and other leaders in the city transferred their allegiance to Jehu.

6. THE HEADS OF THE MEN: As a tangible sign of their surrender, Jehu required the officials to decapitate all of Ahab's male descendants and bring their heads to him the next day.

7. HEADS IN BASKETS: Out of fear, the officials obeyed Jehu by decapitating Ahab's male descendants. However, they did not personally go to Jehu in Jezreel, most likely because they feared a similar fate would await them.

8. TWO HEAPS: It was a common practice in the ancient Near East to pile the heads of conquered subjects at the city gates. The practice was designed to dissuade rebellion.

11. JEHU KILLED ALL: Jehu went beyond God's mandate and executed all of Ahab's officials—a deed for which God would later judge Jehu's house.

13. BROTHERS OF AHAZIAH: These men identifyed themselves as "the brothers of Azaziah." However, according to 2 Chronicles 21:17, the brothers of Ahaziah, the slain king of Judah, had previously been killed by the Philistines, so these must have been relatives of Ahaziah in a broader sense (like nephews and cousins).

14. KILLED THEM AT THE WELL: Jehu killed these forty-two men out of concern they might stimulate and strengthen those who were still loyal to the family of Ahab.

THE END OF BAAL WORSHIP: Jehu completes the work the prophet Elijah had begun by getting rid of all royally sanctioned Baal worship in Israel.

18. AHAB SERVED BAAL A LITTLE, JEHU WILL SERVE HIM MUCH: Jehu promised to outdo Ahab's devotion to Baal as ruse to gather together all the false prophets in the city. The people of Samaria might have thought Jehu was seeking a military reformation rather than a religious one and was thus seeking Baal's blessing on his reign as king.

21. TEMPLE OF BAAL: King Ahab had built this idolatrous worship center in Samaria (see 1 Kings 16:32). All the worshipers could fit into that one edifice because the number of Baal devotees had been reduced by the influence of Elijah and Elisha and by the neglect and discontinuance of Baal worship under Joram.

28. DESTROYED BAAL FROM ISRAEL: Jehu rid the northern kingdom of royally sanctioned Baal worship. However, he did not do this out of spiritual or godly motives, but because he believed Baalism was inextricably bound to the dynasty of Ahab. By exterminating it, he sought to kill last vestiges of Ahab loyalists and incur the support of those who worshiped the true God.

33. FROM THE JORDAN EASTWARD: Because Jehu failed to keep the Lord's law wholeheartedly, God punished him by giving Israel's land east of the Jordan River to Syria. This lost region was the homeland of the tribes of Gad, Reuben, and half of Manasseh.

UNLEASHING THE TEXT

1) Why did Elisha instruct his younger student-prophet to anoint Jehu as king over Israel? What were God's instructions to Jehu that he was to fulfill?

_____

_____

_____

2) How did Jehu ensure that his arrival at Jezreel would be a surprise? How did he fulfill the prophecies that Elijah had made against Ahab and Jezebel?

_____

_____

_____

3) What was Jehu's motivation in destroying the prophets of Baal and their worship site? How would you describe the attitude of Jehu's heart toward the law of God?

_____

_____

_____

4) What happened as a result of Jehu's lack of full devotion to God? What did God say would be the consequences for not walking completely in His ways?

_____

_____

_____

Exploring the Meaning

Those who are obedient to God become part of His plan. There are easier ways for God to accomplish His purposes than to work through the lives of people. Yet God, more often than not, chooses this method. God's purpose is not just to get the work done but also to draw His people back into a faithful relationship with Him.

Elisha heard the word of the Lord concerning God's plan to make Jehu the next king of Israel. His younger student-prophet became a link in that plan by receiving Elisha's instructions and carefully obeying them. Jehu, in turn, received the words of the prophet and immediately responded to make God's plan come to pass. Each of these men became a link in the chain that unfolded God's plan to purge Israel of idol worship and draw His people back to him.

Again and again in the Bible, we see God creating opportunities for the Israelites to live as His faithful people. Those who responded in obedience were rewarded with hearing God's voice and witnessing His miraculous work. They gained knowledge of God as they listened to Him and obeyed His voice. Jesus would later illustrate this relationship when He referred to Himself as the Good Shepherd whose sheep know His voice (see John 10:14). Our relationship with our Shepherd comes from spending time in His presence and following His guidance.

God is faithful to keep His promises. God had spelled out how the house of Ahab would come to an end (see 1 Kings 21:19–24). Ahab and Jezebel had been responsible for pulling the people away from God's laws, leading them into idolatry, and murdering the prophets of the Lord who came to warn them of the consequences of their sin. This evil became a cancer in Israel, and God resolved to remove it from the land.

God used Jehu as the means of bringing to an end the evil that Ahab and Jezebel had brought to Israel. In addition, He not only eliminated the wicked kings of Ahab's line but also all those from his house who could pose a threat of reclaiming the throne. God went on to promise Jehu that his line would rule for four generations. God kept this promise, though He did diminish the kingdom of Israel because Jehu did not completely walk in His ways.

The events in Jehu's story teach us that God takes sin seriously—and that when He makes a promise, He always keeps it. God can be compassionate and forgiving, but he cannot ever lie or go back on His word. "The Lord is not slack concerning His promise, as some count slackness, but is longsuffering toward us, not willing that any should perish but that all should come to repentance. But the day of the Lord will come as a thief in the night" (2 Peter 3:9–10).

God's goal is a faithful people. Sin and pride kept Joram, Ahaziah, and Jehu from experiencing the grace God wanted to extend to them. King Joram of Israel was blind to the consequences of turning from God's laws, and he lost his life and throne as a result. King Ahaziah of Judah did evil in God's sight, and he lost his life and throne at the same time. Jehu responded to God's call to purge Israel and kill the prophets of Baal, but he fell short in his devotion by allowing idolatry to survive. His kingdom was diminished and fell under constant threat from outside enemies.

The Bible tells us that God does not take pleasure in punishing people for their sin. As he said through the prophet Ezekiel, "Do I have any pleasure at all that the wicked should die . . . and not that he should turn from his ways and live?" (Ezekiel 18:23). However, the Bible is equally clear that God will hold people accountable for their sins, and He will use any means He deems necessary to bring people back into relationship with Him. He will use miracles, the pain of our sin, the words of a prophet, or even unbelievers and outside forces to get our attention.

God's desire to bring us back into relationship with Himself was so great that He even willingly sacrificed the life of His only Son as payment for our sins. "For God so loved the world that He gave His only begotten Son, that whoever believes in Him should not perish but have everlasting life. For God did not send His Son into the world to condemn the world, but that the world through Him might be saved" (John 3:16–17). God will not force people to accept this gift, but He will keep working in their lives to bring them back to Him.

REFLECTING ON THE TEXT

5) How was Elisha obedient to God's call? What risks did he take to be obedient? What does this tell us about the risks we may have to take to obey God?

_____

_____

_____

6) How did God fulfill His prophecies concerning Ahab and Jezebel? What message did He send to His people by fulfilling even the minute details of this prophecy?

_____

_____

_____

_____

7) What warnings did God give to the people of Ahab's house before He raised up Jehu to end their line? What opportunities did they have to turn from their wicked ways?

_____

_____

_____

_____

8) How does God seek to bring people today back into relationship with Him? How does He use believers as part of that plan? How can we show we are His faithful people?

_____

_____

_____

_____

PERSONAL RESPONSE

9) What have you felt God calling you to do for His kingdom? What steps are you taking to be faithful in following His ways and to bring others to Christ?

_____

_____

_____

_____

10) What changes do you need to make to be more faithful to what God is calling you to do? How does God's Word help you determine which direction to take?

_____

_____

_____

_____

7

JEHOASH REBUILDS THE TEMPLE
2 Kings 12:1–16

DRAWING NEAR

What are some of the benefits of having a good mentor? What happens in people's lives when they are not surrounded by godly mentors during their childhood years?

_____

_____

_____

THE CONTEXT

Jehoram had become king in Judah after the death of his father, Jehoshaphat, but he had not followed his father's example. He had murdered his brothers when he ascended the throne (to prevent them from trying to take it from him) and had proceeded to lead Judah into paganism. As if this were not enough, he had even married the daughter of Israel's king Ahab and queen Jezebel. Over the years, this woman would cause trouble for Judah, just as her mother had for Israel. The author of Chronicles poignantly summarized Jehoram's reign in this way: "He reigned in Jerusalem eight years and, to no one's sorrow, departed" (2 Chronicles 21:20).

Jehoram's son Ahaziah had assumed the throne after his father's death, but he had only reigned for one year before meeting his end at the hands of Jehu. Following his death, Ahaziah's mother, a woman named Athaliah, seized her opportunity to take the throne of Judah. She quickly set about murdering all her grandchildren so there would be no one left who could displace her by claiming the throne.

Fortunately, there were still godly people left in Judah, including the high priest Jehoiada and his wife, Jehoshabeath. This godly couple rescued Jehoash, one of Ahaziah's sons, and hid him in the temple. During the next six years, Jehoiada instructed young Jehoash in the ways of the Lord, training him to become a godly king who would break the wickedness perpetrated by both his father and grandfather and return the nation to the fear of the Lord. Once Jehoash finally ascended the throne, Jehoiada continued to act as his counselor and mentor, and during those years Jehoash led the people of Judah in righteousness.

KEYS TO THE TEXT

Read 2 Kings 12:1–16, noting the key words and phrases indicated below.

> *JUDAH'S BOY KING: Jehoash is only seven years old when he becomes king of Judah. Jehoiada, the high priest, guides him in the ways of the Lord.*

12.1. JEHOASH BECAME KING: His name, also spelled Joash, means "Yahweh has bestowed." Jehoash became king of Judah in 835 BC (the seventh year of Jehu's reign in Israel) and ruled until 796 BC. Jehoiada's wife, Jehoshabeath, was his aunt.

2. ALL THE DAYS OF JEHOIADA THE PRIEST: Jehoaida had raised Jehoash in the temple and instructed him in God's ways and law. Since he became king at the age of seven, it is likely that Jehoiada also acted as one of his chief advisors for many years.

3. THE HIGH PLACES WERE NOT TAKEN AWAY: As with most kings of Judah, Jehoash failed to remove these places of worship where, contrary to the Mosaic Law, the people sacrificed and burned incense to the Lord. In

2 Chronicles 24:3, we also read that Jehoiada, the high priest, took two wives for him, which was something the Lord had commanded His people *not* to do. This may be an indication that the Lord's commands were gradually being forgotten at this time. Nevertheless, Jehoiada was trying to help Jehoash build a godly family, and he took a strong interest in ensuring the king married Israelite women rather than Canaanites.

REPAIRING THE TEMPLE: *Jehoash sets his heart on repairing the Lord's temple in Jerusalem, but not everyone shares in his zeal.*

4. JEHOASH SAID TO THE PRIESTS: At this point in his reign, Jehoash fully embraced Jehoaida's godly counsel and followed the priorities of God. The fact he set his heart on repairing the temple indicated he had turned his heart toward God and desired to do the things that would please the Lord. This was certainly a direct result of Jehoiada's mentoring.

THE DEDICATED GIFTS: These were offerings given to the priests and used to support the temple. The three offerings listed were the half-shekel assessed from every male twenty years old and above whenever a census was taken (see Exodus 30:11–16); the payments of personal vows (see Leviticus 27:1–8); and voluntary offerings (see Leviticus 22:18–23).

5. HIS CONSTITUENCY: This person could have been a friend of the priest who either gave offerings or collected the offerings for the priest. Some have also interpreted the Hebrew term to mean "treasurer," which would view the individual as a member of the temple personnel who assisted the priests with the valuation of sacrifices and offerings brought to the temple.

REPAIR THE DAMAGES OF THE TEMPLE: The temple had suffered major damages during the reign of Athaliah, whose sons had broken into it and stolen many of the sacred treasures to dedicate them to Baal. (Likely, the dilapidated state of the temple suggests that it had been allowed to fall into disrepair over a long period of time. Syncretism was plaguing both Israel and Judah, and the people had all but abandoned the proper form of worship to the Lord, which was to take place only at the temple.) Jehoash ordered the priests to channel the temple offerings to fund the repairs needed to fix this damage. This was to be in addition to the normal temple expenses.

6. THE PRIESTS HAD NOT REPAIRED THE DAMAGES: Jehoash had made it clear the temple repairs were a priority, but the priests (Levites) had not

complied. We are not told why they failed to repair the temple, but the author's tone suggests they did not share the king's desire to renew the Lord's house of worship. Apparently, Jehoiada did not instill in his fellow Levites the same heart for God that he had taught to the king.

7. NEITHER RECEIVE MORE MONEY . . . NOR REPAIR: The priests would no longer receive the offerings from the people or fund the temple repairs from the income they had received.

TAKING A COLLECTION: Jehoash's plan has failed, so he turns to the people of Judah directly to help support the effort to rebuild the temple. The response is overwhelming.

9. JEHOIADA THE PRIEST TOOK A CHEST: Jehoash's new plan was to set up a single collection box in the temple to receive all incoming offerings. When the chest was full, the royal secretary and high priest would empty it and, from the funds generated, hire men to supervise and pay the carpenters, builders, masons, and stonecutters who worked on the temple repairs. The men involved were so trustworthy that no accounting was taken.

9. PRIESTS WHO KEPT THE DOOR: These priests, who normally screened the people to keep unclean worshipers from entering the temple, took the offerings from the worshipers. They then personally watched the priests drop the offerings into the chest.

10. WHENEVER THEY SAW THAT THERE WAS MUCH MONEY IN THE CHEST: The Mosaic Law prescribed some of the monetary contributions, but the use of the chest also permitted freewill offerings. The people of Judah were evidently eager to participate in the temple's renewal, and much of the cost was funded through such voluntary giving. What is particularly striking is that the money was given with a spirit of rejoicing. There was evidently no begrudging the contributions, as all the people eagerly took part in restoring the Lord's place of worship.

11. THE HANDS OF THOSE WHO DID THE WORK: Everyone in Judah participated in this great renewal project. Some used the skills the Lord had given them to do the work, while others provided the finances needed to carry it out.

16. MONEY FROM THE TRESPASS OFFERINGS AND . . . SIN OFFERINGS: The income from these offerings was distinct from the income mentioned in 2 Kings 12:4. For this reason, it was not used in the repair of the temple but

remained the property of the priests. The temple repairs did not deprive the priests of their income.

GOING DEEPER

The author of Chronicles gives us some details about Jehoash's reign not found in the book of Kings. Read 2 Chronicles 24:16–22, noting the key words and phrases indicated below.

THE DEATH OF JEHOIADA: *The high priest dies, leaving the king without a counselor. Jehoash soon leads the people back into idolatry.*

15. BUT JEHOIADA GREW OLD: The word *but* brings the reader up short in these verses and indicates there was about to be an abrupt change. As long as Jehoiada was involved in Jehoash's life, the people worshiped the Lord continually. However, after his death the situation in Judah would begin to deteriorate once again.

16. THEY BURIED HIM . . . AMONG THE KINGS: This was a high honor, as there is no record of any other high priest being buried among the kings. It indicates the people of Judah recognized the godly influence that Jehoiada had exercised on the reign of their king. They apparently ascribed to him the spiritual renewal that had taken place. Subsequent events would demonstrate that this was indeed the case.

17. THE KINGS LISTENED TO THEM: It appears that Jehoash had never learned how to take the principles taught by his mentor and apply them for himself. He had evidently relied heavily on Jehoiada's counsel, and when the high priest was no longer available, he turned to others for guidance. It is significant these counselors were the *leaders* of Judah, not just some random friends. The previous suppression of these leaders indicates the strong leadership that Jehoiada had exercised during his time as high priest, for these political leaders were evidently opposed to his determination to restore correct worship practices in Judah.

18. THEY LEFT THE HOUSE OF THE LORD GOD: The people of Judah had incorporated pagan practices into their worship for so long that it seemed strange to them when they were called to return to obedience to the Lord. The leadership

of Judah may well have considered Jehoiada a sort of fanatic who insisted on old-fashioned and outdated worship. Once he was out of the way, they went back to inventing their own worship practices and disregarding God's Word.

19. HE SENT PROPHETS TO THEM: Once again we see the Lord's patience and long-suffering toward His people's persistent disobedience. Their wickedness stirred up His wrath, yet He stayed His hand in mercy and extended grace to them by continuing to send prophets to lead them back into obedience.

21. STONED HIM WITH STONES IN THE COURT OF THE HOUSE OF THE LORD: At the express command of Jehoash, the wicked leaders of Judah defiled the temple court by murdering Jehoiada's own son in that place. Jehoash's reign had begun well, but it ended in the darkest disgrace. His treachery was later repaid when his own servants conspired to murder him.

UNLEASHING THE TEXT

1) Why did Jehoiada and his wife take such great risks to save Jehoash's life? What was the result of their selfless acts?

_____

_____

_____

2) Why did Jehoash set his heart on rebuilding the temple? How had the temple fallen into disrepair? Why did the priests not obey the king's commands?

_____

_____

_____

_____

3) What motivated the people of Judah to give so generously to the rebuilding project? How does their example apply to God's people today?

_____

_____

_____

4) Why did Jehoash forget what he owed Jehoiada's family? Why did he have Jehoiada's son murdered? What should he have done instead?

_____

_____

_____

EXPLORING THE MEANING

Train the next generation to faithfully serve the Lord. We have seen many mentors in the course of these studies. Elijah trained Elisha. Elisha trained Gehazi. Jehoiada trained Jehoash. Some of these mentoring relationships were more effective than others, but they all have some things in common. First, there was always a close relationship between mentor and pupil. In these examples, the men actually lived together and spent their waking hours working together. Second, the mentor's training included both practical experience and theoretical reaching. Elisha gave Gehazi opportunities to interact with others and develop a heart for their needs. Jehoiada set Jehoash on the throne where he took on the affairs of overseeing a nation.

One critical step in this process is that mentor trains the pupil to rely on God rather than on human counselors. Elisha learned this important lesson, and it enabled him to take over his mentor's responsibilities once Elijah's ministry was completed. Jehoash did not learn this critical lesson, and it destroyed what had begun as a godly career as king. Apparently Jehoash never went beyond relying on Jehoiada for direction and counsel. He never learned how to serve the Lord and rely on His Word. This step is vital, as illustrated in Jehoash's life, because it is at the core of Christian mentorship. Teaching others to be faithful servants requires teaching them how to draw close to God themselves.

God's original structure for the mentoring process was the family. It is no coincidence in Scripture that the disciple frequently refers to his mentor as "father," for God intended human fathers to be loving mentors to their entire families. "These words which I command you today shall be in your heart. You shall teach them diligently to your children, and shall talk of them when you sit in your house, when you walk by the way, when you lie down, and when you rise up" (Deuteronomy 6:6–7). Notice the process: we are to keep His Word in our heart, teach it diligently, and talk about God's Word during daily activities. When God's people follow this pattern, they effectively train the next generation to walk in the ways of the Lord and also teach them by example to do the same for their own children.

Avoid the sin of ingratitude. King Jehoash owed a great deal to the spiritual leadership of Jehoiada—indeed, he owed very his life to the high priest and his wife. Yet Jehoiada's gifts did not end with the preservation of Jehoash's life, for the high priest undoubtedly taught the young boy from the Word of God during the years he was living at the temple. Jehoiada later gathered the people together and made Jehoash king, again at great risk to himself, and continued to counsel him in the ways of righteousness.

But Jehoash "did not remember the kindness which Jehoiada his father had done to him" (2 Chronicles 24:22), and this same forgetfulness led him into a great sin. How could a man forget such costly and selfless love, especially when he owed his kingship and his life to the man who had been like a father to him? The answer is found in the heart of every human being. Jehoash fell into ingratitude because he forgot to remember the goodness God had shown to him. We also fall into ingratitude when we fail to remember the goodness of God.

Gratitude requires effort on our part to remember the blessings we have received through the efforts of others. This is the reason the Bible commands us to deliberately remember all the Lord has done on our behalf, for without such deliberate recollection, we will quickly take His love and kindness for granted. As King David wrote, "Bless the LORD, O my soul, and forget not all His benefits" (Psalm 103:2). This is done by choosing to rejoice rather than complain, by intentionally focusing on a spirit of thankfulness, and by taking our gratitude directly to God. Paul wrote, "Rejoice always, pray without ceasing, in everything give thanks; for this is the will of God in Christ Jesus for you" (1 Thessalonians 5:16–18).

The Lord loves a cheerful giver. King Jehoash commanded the Levites to oversee repairs to the temple in Jerusalem. This was an important priority for God's people—but the Levites did not obey. They did not rebel openly but simple refused make it a priority because they lacked any zeal for the project. So Jehoash placed a "donations chest" outside the temple and called on the people of Judah to donate voluntarily—and the people responded with the zeal that the priests lacked. In fact, their gifts amounted to more than what was required, as they poured out their contributions with an open hand.

This kind of generosity grows out of a spirit of gratitude. When we remember to be grateful for everything the Lord has done, we naturally respond by giving to Him—and that spirit delights the heart of God. The opposite of this is also true, for when we have a spirit of ingratitude, we are less likely to joyfully give of our time and resources. The one feeds the other. A spirit of gratitude prompts us to give generously, and when we give generously, the Lord blesses us generously, giving us yet more for which to be grateful.

The Lord is not a hard taskmaster and does not demand a heavy tax burden from His people. Indeed, the opportunity to give to His work on earth is yet another of His blessings, for it allows each of us to take part in His work throughout the earth. When we give generously, He has promised to give us even greater blessings—which in turn will enable us to continue giving generously. Paul taught, "He who sows sparingly will also reap sparingly, and he who sows bountifully will also reap bountifully. So let each one give as he purposes in his heart, not grudgingly or of necessity; for God loves a cheerful giver" (2 Corinthians 9:6–7).

REFLECTING ON THE TEXT

5) Why did Judah revert to paganism so quickly after Jehoiada's death? What does this suggest about the spiritual condition of the priests at the time?

_____

_____

_____

_____

6) What practical lessons can you glean from the various mentors in these studies? (Consider Elijah/Elisha, Elisha/Gehazi, Jehoiada/Jehoash, and others.)

_____

_____

_____

_____

_____

7) What sin is at the root of an ungrateful spirit? How can a Christian cultivate a generous spirit? Why is this important?

_____

_____

_____

_____

8) Who has been a mentor in your life? Who might list you as a mentor in his or her life? Whom might the Lord want you to mentor in the future?

_____

_____

_____

_____

_____

Personal Response

9) Do you tend to give cheerfully or begrudgingly? How can you cultivate a more generous spirit in the future?

_____

_____

_____

_____

10) What are at least ten things for which you are thankful? List these below, and then spend time in prayer thanking the Lord for His countless blessings in your life.

_____

_____

_____

_____

8

THE FALL OF ISRAEL

2 Kings 17:1–33

DRAWING NEAR

What are some problems that arise when a government or other form of
power tries to relocate a group of people from one place to another?

_____

_____

_____

THE CONTEXT

The monarchy of the ten northern tribes had been a troubled one ever since
the unified kingdom of Israel split into two under Rehoboam. For more than
200 years since that break, Israel had been ruled by a succession of kings who
were not faithful to God's commands. Some of these rulers, like Ahab and
Jezebel, were so wicked that God decreed their descendants would never sit on
the throne. Israel became increasingly idolatrous, until it was virtually indis-
tinguishable from the pagan nations around it.

After Jehu came to power, the Lord promised that four generations of his
sons would rule Israel (see 2 Kings 10:30). None of these kings—Jehoahaz,

Jehoash, Jeroboam II, or Zechariah—walked in the ways of the Lord, and ultimately the throne went to a usurper named Shallum. He reigned only a month before a man named Manahem killed him. During his reign, the powerful Assyrians invaded and were only turned back when Manahem offered them tribute, which made Israel into a vassal state of the Assyrian king. Manahem's son Pekahiah then ruled for two years before an outsider named Pekah overthrew him, and he in turn was overthrown in a conspiracy led by a man named Hoshea.

As we will see in this study, Hoshea would prove to be a foolish king who foolishly tried to ally with the Egyptians. The result was Hoshea's imprisonment and an Assyrian siege against Samaria. By 722 BC, the Assyrians had conquered all of Israel and carried its people into slavery in foreign lands. The author of Kings sums up the sad reason for these events: "For so it was that the children of Israel had sinned against the LORD their God. . . . Therefore the LORD was very angry with Israel, and removed them from His sight" (2 Kings 17:7, 18).

KEYS TO THE TEXT

Read 2 Kings 17:1–33, noting the key words and phrases indicated below.

> THE SINS OF ISRAEL: *For more than 100 years the people of Israel have been chasing after foreign gods. The Lord's patience with them has finally come to an end.*

17:1. IN THE TWELFTH YEAR OF AHAZ: The date for Hoshea's accession (732 BC) is well established according to biblical and extrabiblical data. Therefore, Ahaz of Judah must have become co-regent with his father Jotham, who was himself co-regent with his father, Azariah, at that time. Hoshea would reign for nine years, until 722 BC, according to the accession-year system.

2. HE DID EVIL: Although Hoshea was characterized as a wicked king, it is not stated that he promoted the religious practices of Jeroboam I. In this way, he was some improvement over the kings of Israel who had gone before him. However, this did not offset the centuries of sin by Israel's kings or divert the nation's inevitable doom.

3. SHALMANESER KING OF ASSYRIA: Shalmaneser V succeeded his father, Tiglath-Pileser III, as king of Assyria and reigned from 727–722 BC. He

died during the siege of Samaria, when the Assyrians began the destruction and captivity of the northern kingdom, and was succeeded by Sargon II. This king completed the siege, captured the city, destroyed Israel, and exiled the inhabitants. Sargon II reigned as king from 722–705 BC.

4. SO, KING OF EGYPT: Instead of paying his yearly tribute owed as a vassal of Assyria, Hoshea tried to make a treaty with Osorkon IV (c. 727–716 BC), king of Egypt. This was foolish, because Assyria was powerful. It was also against God's will, which forbade such alliances with pagan rulers (see Deuteronomy 7:2). This rebellion led directly to Israel's destruction.

5. WENT UP TO SAMARIA AND BESIEGED IT FOR THREE YEARS: Shalmaneser V invaded Israel and quickly conquered the land, but the capital city of Samaria resisted the Assyrian invaders until 722 BC. Like all major cities, Samaria had an internal water supply and plenty of stored food that allowed her to endure the siege for three years.

6. CARRIED ISRAEL AWAY: The capture of Samaria marked the end of the northern kingdom. According to Assyrian records, the Assyrians deported 27,290 inhabitants of Israel to distant locations. These Israelites were resettled in the upper Tigris-Euphrates Valley and never again returned to the Promised Land. (Halah was a city northeast of Nineveh, the Habor River was a northern tributary of the Euphrates, and the "cities of the Medes" were northeast of Nineveh.) Some of the Jews were carried as far east as Susa, where the events of the book of Esther would take place. In this way, God fulfilled what He had promised to His people if they did not follow Him: "The LORD will scatter you among all peoples" (Deuteronomy 28:64).

THE CAUSE OF THE EXILE: The author of Kings interrupts his narrative to comment on what had led to Israel's conquest by the Assyrians and the people's exile.

7. THEY HAD FEARED OTHER GODS. The primary cause of Israel's exile was the worship of other gods. The fear of the Lord led to listening to His Word and obeying His ordinances and statutes, but the fear of the gods of Canaan led Israel to obey the laws of the Canaanite gods.

8. WALKED IN THE STATUES OF THE NATIONS: This included idolatry and pagan worship in the high places, but it also included other abominations, such as child sacrifice and astrology. Israel, as we shall see, was guilty of

practically every atrocity the Canaanites had practiced before Israel's arrival in the Promised Land—and for which the Lord had driven out the Canaanites in the first place. That same fate was now coming on the northern tribes of Israel.

AND OF THE KINGS OF ISRAEL: As we have seen, Israel's king Jeroboam I had attempted to rewrite God's prescribed worship practices in Israel. He had led the people to worship the Lord at a variety of sites around Israel, rather than in Jerusalem, as the Lord had commanded. He had also added an idolatrous element to their worship by introducing the golden calves. The people of Israel were guilty of open idolatry and also of syncretism—the sin of mixing pagan practices into legitimate worship of God.

9. ISRAEL SECRETLY DID AGAINST THE LORD: The Hebrew word translated *secretly* literally means "to cover." The people of Israel thought they could hide their wicked deeds from the Lord, as though such a thing were possible. In addition to their private sins, judgment came for their public wickedness and idolatry.

BUILT FOR THEMSELVES HIGH PLACES: These were not the high places the Israelites used for worshiping God before the building of the temple. In direct disobedience to God's commands in Deuteronomy 12:1–4, the Israelites built new, raised altars in the Canaanite pattern after the temple was constructed. These high places were in all the habitations of Israel, from small fortified structures to large garrison cities

10. SACRED PILLARS AND WOODEN IMAGES: The wooden images were carved representations of false gods, while the pillars were fertility objects used during rituals involving sexual immorality. These objects of wickedness were spread throughout the northern tribes and were found "on every high hill and under every green tree."

11. LIKE THE NATIONS WHOM THE LORD HAD CARRIED AWAY BEFORE THEM: Once again, we are reminded the Lord had driven out the Canaanites from the land for these very same practices. If He drove out the Canaanites for such wickedness, He would surely also drive out the Israelites.

> THE LORD'S LONG-SUFFERING: *Despite the people's sin, the Lord had continued to send prophets to urge them to repentance. Yet the people had refused to turn back to Him.*

12. YOU SHALL NOT DO THIS THING: God had commanded His people, "You shall not make for yourself a carved image—any likeness of anything that

is in heaven above, or that is in the earth beneath, or that is in the water under the earth; you shall not bow down to them nor serve them" (Exodus 20:4–5).

13. TURN FROM YOUR EVIL WAYS: Despite the widespread paganism in Israel, the Lord continued to give His people opportunities to repent. He sent prophets to Israel and Judah, never left them without spiritual guidance, and urged them continuously to turn away from idolatry and back to Him. But the people became obstinate, insisting on doing things their own way regardless of what God commanded.

15. THEY REJECTED HIS STATUTES AND HIS COVENANT: The Lord had taught His people how to worship Him and live according to His will through the teachings of His prophets, including Moses, and the covenants He had made, which promised them blessings if they obeyed His commands. Yet the people had preferred to imitate the world around them. The church today is in danger of doing the same thing, as many attempt to incorporate all manner of worldly values and ideas into their worship practices under the cloak of being "relevant" to the world around them. In reality, such syncretism only makes the church worldly, not relevant.

THEY SHOULD NOT DO LIKE THEM: God commanded His people to be different from the world. If God's church is just like every other worldly organization, the unsaved have no reason to go there. Paradoxically, it is our very difference from the world around us that draws sinners to Christ, for only then can they see that God alone is the source of salvation.

16. TWO CALVES . . . WOODEN IMAGE . . . THE HOST OF HEAVEN: Jeroboam I had led Israel to worship the golden calves (see 1 Kings 12:25–33), while Rehoboam had built the wooden image (see 1 Kings 14:15). The people also committed the sin of astrology, looking to the stars for guidance instead of to God's Word.

17. TO PASS THROUGH THE FIRE, PRACTICED WITCHCRAFT AND SOOTHSAYING: The Canaanites believed in a god named Molech, whose worship included sacrificing children in the fire. Witchcraft includes the sin of attempting to contact the spirit world and to use magic to control the natural realm. Soothsaying is the sin of divination, or endeavoring to use magical means to foretell the future. Latent in this is the idea that the dead can guide better than God's Word.

SOLD THEMSELVES TO DO EVIL: This phrase captures the essence of sin. Just as Esau sold his birthright to Jacob in exchange for a bowl of stew, and

Adam sold himself into slavery to sin and death in exchange for a piece of fruit, so men and women sell their souls in exchange for worthless, momentary pleasures. Sin is always a bad bargain.

> THE NEW SETTLERS: *After the people of Israel are removed from the land, the Assyrians bring in people from across their empire to resettle the territory.*

22. THE SINS OF JEROBOAM: The sins of that king put into motion an unbroken pattern of idolatrous iniquity in the ten northern tribes of Israel.

23. AS IT IS TO THIS DAY: The exiles of Israel would never return *en masse*, as did Judah would later do under the Persians.

24. THE KING OF ASSYRIA BROUGHT PEOPLE: After the Assyrian conquest, they made the central hill and coastal plain regions of the former northern kingdom an Assyrian province, all of which was called "Samaria" after the ancient capital city. Sargon II settled alien people, who came from widely scattered areas also conquered by Assyria, in the abandoned Israelite towns.

BABYLON, CUTHAH, AVA, HAMATH, AND FROM SEPHARVAIM: Babylon and Cuthah were located in southern Mesopotamia. Hamath was a town on the Orontes River in Syria. The exact location of Ava and Sepharvaim are unknown. These people, who intermarried with the Jews who escaped exile, became the Samaritans—a mixed Jew and Gentile people, later hated by the Jews in the New Testament (see Matthew 10:5; Luke 10:29–36; John 4:9).

> LION TROUBLE: *It isn't long before the settlers—who have brought their pagan gods with them into Israel—encounter some unusual trouble and turn to the Assyrian king for help.*

25. LIONS AMONG THEM: God occasionally employed lions as instruments of divine punishment (see 1 Kings 13:24; 20:36).

26. THE RITUALS OF THE GOD OF THE LAND: The newcomers interpreted the lions as a punishment from the God of Israel, whom they viewed as a deity who needed to be placated. They did not know how to appease Him, so they appealed to Sargon II for help. In response, the Assyrian king

ordered an exiled Israelite priest to go back to Samaria to teach the people what the God of the land required in worship.

29. EVERY NATION CONTINUED TO MAKE GODS OF ITS OWN: The new residents were taught the proper way to worship God, but they continued to place Yahweh alongside their other gods in an eclectic kind of worship. This was blasphemy to the one true and living God.

30. SUCCOTH BENOTH . . . NERGAL . . . ASHIMA . . . NIBHAZ AND TARTAK: These were the names of the gods the new residents fashioned into the form of idols. Succoth Benoth literally means "tents of the daughters" and was probably a deity worshiped by sexual orgies. Nergal was perhaps the Assyrian god of war. Ashima was an idol in the form of a bald male goat. Nibhaz was a dog-like idol. Tartak was either a donkey or a celestial body (Saturn).

ADRAMMELECH AND ANAMMELECH: Adrammelech was perhaps the same as Molech, worshiped in the form of the sun, a mule, or a peacock. Anammelech was a rabbit or goat idol.

33. SERVED THEIR OWN GODS: The religion of the Samaritans was syncretistic. They combined elements of the worship of the Lord with the worship practices of the gods whom they had brought with them.

UNLEASHING THE TEXT

1) What does it mean to walk "in the statutes of the nations" (2 Kings 17:8)? What are some statutes of modern nations that differ from the Word of God?

2) What does it mean that the people of Israel "stiffened their necks" against the Lord (verse 14)? How does a person become stiff-necked? How does one stop being stiff-necked?

_____

_____

_____

3) Why does God view divination as such an extreme example of sin? When someone turns to such things for guidance, what does that say about their trust in God's Word?

_____

_____

_____

4) What happened when the Assyrians resettled into Israel conquered people from other places in their empire? Why did God send lions among them?

_____

_____

_____

Exploring the Meaning

God's judgment is coming. The Lord endured the unfaithfulness of His people for centuries. The ten northern tribes of Israel committed all manner of wickedness, chasing after gods that didn't exist and imitating the pagan nations around them, yet the Lord stayed His hand of judgment. Even more, He sent prophets and teachers to call them to repentance and teach them the true ways of righteousness. Yet God's people rejected those prophets, mocking them and imprisoning them and murdering them—all the time persisting in their idolatrous practices.

The prophets warned the people of Israel that the Lord's wrath would come on them if they did not repent, but the people did not believe. As we have seen in previous studies, the Lord always keeps His promises—and this includes vows of coming judgment. After several hundred years of stubborn indulgence in sin, God finally drove His people out of Canaan. Countless Israelites were slaughtered, while those who survived faced slavery and hardship for the rest of their days. Yet no one in Israel could accuse God of treachery, for He had warned them again and again of the judgment that would come if they did not repent.

We live today in the age of God's grace, but we must never forget that this time of grace will come to an end—and it will be followed by God's final judgment on the sinfulness of mankind. The captivity and suffering of Israel will be nothing compared to this coming judgment, when those who have refused to repent will be cast into outer darkness—not for a lifetime but for all eternity. Those who accept God's gift of salvation will not face that judgment, yet even Christians must never take God's grace for granted or test His patience with continual sin. Paul had this in mind when he urged his readers, "We . . . plead with you not to receive the grace of God in vain. For He says: 'In an acceptable time I have heard you, and in the day of salvation I have helped you.' Behold, now is the accepted time; behold, now is the day of salvation" (2 Corinthians 6:1–2).

God sees all things, and nothing is done in secret. The people of Israel grew bold in their idolatries, carrying out their false worship on open hilltops and public groves, and these rites frequently included all sorts of evil. However, they did not limit their sinful behaviors to just these idolatrous ceremonies but carried their spiritual rebellion into the most secret areas of their private lives. They were undoubtedly able to hide such things from their friends and neighbors, but they were foolish in thinking they could keep them secret from the Lord.

The Israelites may also have covered their sins in a cloak of respectability, using false logic to argue their sin wasn't actually sin at all. Humans are very skilled in such sophistry and are able to justify every sinful deed to the point of calling evil good and good evil. But God hates such a mindset, as He warned us through the prophet Isaiah: "Woe to those who call evil good, and good evil; who put darkness for light, and light for darkness; who put bitter for sweet, and sweet for bitter!" (Isaiah 5:20).

There is nothing hidden from God's sight, and that includes both our deeds and our elaborate excuses to justify our sins. Paul wrote that the Lord "will both bring to light the hidden things of darkness and reveal the counsels of the hearts" (1 Corinthians 4:5). When we remember that God sees our hearts and our secret actions, we will be more likely to walk circumspectly and more quick to confess our sins. However, when we try to keep those sins secret, we will act foolishly, "for there is nothing covered that will not be revealed, nor hidden that will not be known" (Luke 12:2).

Occult activities are an attempt to replace God. The idolatry of Israel began as syncretism, but it ended with the most hideous abominations, including child sacrifice. This was a clear testimony that the Israelites thought the one true God was insufficient to guide them and they needed protection and direction from other gods. While child sacrifice may sound like an extreme case, the fact is that all disobedience to God's Word eventually leads to abominable practices if we do not repent and turn away from disobedience.

By definition, sin is the act of choosing to follow inner desires rather than submitting to God, and all sin leads inexorably away from the Lord and toward evil. Interestingly, the Lord includes child sacrifice in the category of occult abominations. Today this is practiced through the widespread sin of abortion. It is no coincidence that as Western civilization hardens its heart against God, sins like these are becoming more accepted.

Christians, of course, must have no part in this. God strictly forbade His people to even associate with "anyone who makes his son or his daughter pass through the fire, or one who practices witchcraft, or a soothsayer, or one who interprets omens, or a sorcerer, or one who conjures spells, or a medium, or a spiritist, or one who calls up the dead. For all who do these things are an abomination to the LORD, and because of these abominations the LORD your God drives them out from before you" (Deuteronomy 18:10–12). As Christians, our direction and protection is found in the Lord, not through other means such as the sacrifice of children.

REFLECTING ON THE TEXT

5) What does it mean to sell oneself to do evil (see 2 Kings 17:17)? How does this happen? How does one prevent it?

_____

_____

_____

_____

6) What did God do to prevent His people from losing the Promised Land? What did the people do to thwart Him? What was the result?

_____

_____

_____

_____

_____

7) Why does God hate the occult? Why does He forbid His people to even associate with those who practice such things?

_____

_____

_____

_____

8) In what ways does sin breed more sin? When have you seen this in your own life? What is the solution to breaking out of that cycle?

_____

_____

_____

_____

PERSONAL RESPONSE

9) Are you trusting in your own righteousness or the righteousness of Jesus Christ to reconcile you to God? (Understand that you can be forgiven by turning to Christ as your Savior and Lord through repentance and faith.)

_____

_____

_____

_____

10) Are you harboring secret sins in your life? What false reasoning are you using to justify such sins? Are you willing to openly confess those things to the Lord today?

_____

_____

_____

9

HEZEKIAH'S STAND

2 Kings 18:1–19:37

DRAWING NEAR

Why is propaganda such an effective tool in creating fear and doubt in people? What are some ways that people use propaganda in media to sway others to their viewpoints?

_____

_____

_____

THE CONTEXT

The kingdom of Israel had fallen to the powerful Assyrian Empire, but the kingdom of Judah still remained in the south. After the promising rule of Jehoash ended in failure, his descendants Amaziah, Uzziah (also called Azariah), and Jotham all did what was right in God's eyes, though they did not tear down the pagan worship sites in Judah. After the death of King Jotham, his son Ahaz came to the throne, and he led the people into wickedness.

Ahaz worshiped Molech, the god of the Moabites, and was the first king in the line of David since Solomon to personally make sacrifices at the high places. However, when his son Hezekiah came to power, he broke that pattern and turned his heart toward the Lord. The Bible tells us that Judah had never had a king like Hezekiah either before or after his time (see 2 Kings 18:5). He went farther in righteousness than any of Judah's other good kings by tearing down the high places that had plagued the nation for generations.

In the history of the Israelites, God would often bless obedience with times of peace and prosperity. Yet God, in His sovereignty, had a different plan for Hezekiah. In the fourth year of his reign, the nation of Israel was attacked and taken into captivity by Assyria. Eight years later, Assyria also attacked Judah, intending to do with them as they had done with Israel. This illustrates the fact that God does permit His people to face trials and hardship. Such situations do not necessarily indicate that the Lord is angry with His people—there are times when He chooses to use difficult circumstances to increase our faith and grow us in blessings.

This was the case with Hezekiah, who faced one of the most dangerous times in Judah's history. The nation's fate hung in the balance, but King Hezekiah knew how to respond. He took the burden to the Lord and trusted Him to fight the battle.

Keys to the Text

Read 2 Kings 18:1–19:37, noting the key words and phrases indicated below.

> *Hezekiah's Reforms: Hezekiah is young when he comes to the throne, but the reforms he implements in Judah show he is wise beyond his years.*

18:1. THIRD YEAR OF HOSHEA: King Hoshea of Israel began to reign in 732 BC, which means Hezekiah began his reign in 729 BC. He was co-regent with his father, Ahaz, until 715 BC.

2. HE REIGNED TWENTY-NINE YEARS: Hezekiah reigned by himself for twenty years (715–695 BC) and with his son, Manasseh, for nine years (695–686 BC). The twenty-nine years given here indicate only those years after his co-regency with Ahaz was over, when he was the actual sovereign. During Hezekiah's reign, the prophets Isaiah and Micah ministered in Judah.

4. REMOVED THE HIGH PLACES: Hezekiah was the first king of Judah to eradicate the high places (the worship centers built contrary to the Law of Moses). He even destroyed the idols used in the worship of Baal and Asherah.

THE BRONZE SERPENT: This was the bronze snake, called the Nehushtan, which God told Moses to make to protect the Israelites from dying of snakebites (see Numbers 21:6–9). The people of Judah—perhaps influenced by Canaanites religions that regarded snakes as fertility symbols—had come to worship it as an idol. Hezekiah smashed it into pieces.

5. HE TRUSTED IN THE LORD GOD OF ISRAEL. The noblest quality of Hezekiah—in contrast to his father—was his reliance on the Lord as his exclusive hope in every situation. What would distinguish him from all other kings of Judah was his firm trust in the Lord during a national crisis. Despite troublesome events, Hezekiah clung tightly to the Lord, faithfully following Him and obeying His commands. As a result, the Lord was with him and gave him success.

THE ASSYRIAN THREAT: When Hezekiah boldly asserts his nation's independence, King Sennacherib of Assyria retaliates and demands an outrageous tribute from Judah.

7. HE REBELLED AGAINST THE KING OF ASSYRIA: Hezekiah's father had submitted to Assyria, but Hezekiah courageously broke that control and asserted Judah's independence.

8. AS FAR AS GAZA: This was the southernmost city of the Philistines, located about fifty-five miles southwest of Jerusalem. Assyria controlled Philistia, which meant Hezekiah's invasion defied Assyrian rule and brought the threat of retaliation.

11. ASSYRIA CARRIED ISRAEL AWAY CAPTIVE: The author of Kings flashes back to the time just before the kingdom of Israel's captivity as a graphic reminder of the threat Assyria posed to Judah. The review sets the scene for the siege of Jerusalem with its reminder of Israel's apostasy, against which Hezekiah's faith in the Lord was a bright contrast.

13. THE FOURTEENTH YEAR OF KING HEZEKIAH: Eight years after the Assyrians conquered Israel, they turned their attention to the destruction of Judah as well.

14. I HAVE DONE WRONG: It was not the Lord's will for His people to submit to Assyria's tyranny, as He had commanded the Israelites to make no covenants with the Gentile nations (see Deuteronomy 7:2). When Hezekiah first took the throne, he boldly threw off the yoke of servitude to Assyria that his father had established. Unfortunately, even Hezekiah gave in under the pressure of the Assyrian army and tried to rectify the situation by paying tribute.

WHATEVER YOU IMPOSE ON ME I WILL PAY: Sennacherib asked for about eleven tons of silver and one ton of gold. To pay this, Hezekiah emptied the temple and palace treasuries and stripped the layers of gold off the doors and doorposts of the temple. Unfortunately, despite Hezekiah's efforts, Sennacherib still demanded Judah's surrender.

TAUNTS AND BOASTS: Sennacherib sends messengers from Assyria to stand outside Judah's walls and attempt to sow discord and fear.

17. THE TARTAN, THE RABSARIS, AND THE RABSHAKEH: These were titles for the general of the Assyrian army, a high-ranking court official, and a field commander respectively.

19. WHAT CONFIDENCE IS THIS IN WHICH YOU TRUST: The Rabshakeh essentially said, "Just who do you think you are, rebelling against Assyria?" His words suggest they viewed Hezekiah's rebellion as an open declaration that he had faith in his God. The Assyrians took this as an affront to *their* gods, for Hezekiah was effectively saying that his God was greater than theirs.

22. HE WHOSE HIGH PLACES AND WHOSE ALTARS HEZEKIAH HAS TAKEN AWAY: The irony is that it was *not* the Lord's altars that were removed from the high places, but the syncretistic shrines we have encountered throughout these studies. The Rabshakeh's speech was an early example of enemy propaganda during wartime, designed to cause division and strife within Judah.

23. TO PUT RIDERS ON THEM: The Assyrian turned his taunts from Judah's God to Judah's military, pointing out they lacked both weapons and the men to wield them. It is unlikely Judah had any chariot forces, and the Israelites as a whole generally fought on foot rather than on horseback. Assyria's military might was vastly superior to Judah's—but King Hezekiah knew better than to rely on anything other than God.

25. THE LORD SAID TO ME: The Assyrian speaker concluded his masterpiece of propaganda by referring to the prophecies of Isaiah, in which the

Lord had warned His people that He would send the Assyrians against them (see Isaiah 8:7–8). The Rabshakeh was essentially telling the people his army was there to fulfill that prophecy, and his words undoubtedly struck fear in the hearts of God's people.

26. DO NOT SPEAK TO US IN HEBREW: The educated people throughout Canaan spoke Aramaic, while Hebrew was the language of the Jews. The Assyrians chose to speak in Hebrew rather than Aramaic for that very reason: they wanted the Jews to understand their words in the hopes of creating fear and insurrection within Judah. This is the tactic the devil uses, even today, for he is always working to cause division and strife among God's people.

29. DO NOT LET HEZEKIAH DECEIVE YOU: This taunt inadvertently gave high praise to King Hezekiah, as it demonstrated his commitment to the Lord was known even in the pagan world. It also showed that Hezekiah had urged his people to trust in the Lord.

32. THE LORD WILL DELIVER US: In this masterpiece of twisted logic, the Assyrians claimed they were coming as God's tool of judgment on His people, while simultaneously urging the people to not trust in Him. The devil loves to twist God's Word, which is why it is important for Christians to know how to rightly divide the word of truth (see 2 Timothy 2:15).

36. THE PEOPLE HELD THEIR PEACE: This statement demonstrates the effective leadership of King Hezekiah, for the people remained silent out of obedience to his command. It is also a good example of how to respond to the devil's arguments, for there are times when the best response is no response.

HEZEKIAH'S RESPONSE: *Instead of arguing with the Assyrians in the face their threats, King Hezekiah decides to turn to the Lord for an answer.*

19:1. WENT INTO THE HOUSE OF THE LORD: Hezekiah had commanded the people not to respond to the Assyrians' defiance, but the king did respond—by going before the Lord.

2. ISAIAH THE PROPHET: This is the first reference in the books of Kings to one of the Lord's greatest prophets. By this time he had already been ministering in Judah for forty years.

3. TROUBLE, AND REBUKE, AND BLASPHEMY: Hezekiah enumerated three sources of evil in this statement. The people were facing trouble, which

refs to any problem caused by an external source, but they were also facing the Lord's deliberate rebuke. In this, Hezekiah acknowledged the Lord had just cause against the people of Judah for their many years of unfaithfulness. But the third source of evil was Rabshakeh's blasphemous words, which urged God's people to remove their faith from Him and place it in the strength and kindly intentions of the Assyrians. Hezekiah called on the Lord to turn His rebuke against the Assyrians for their blasphemy.

6. DO NOT BE AFRAID: Through the prophet Isaiah, the Lord commanded the people of Judah not to yield to fear. The Assyrians were counting on the people's fear to drive them directly into their hands, just as the devil uses fear to drive people into his nets of destruction.

HEZEKIAH'S PRAYER: The king takes Sennacherib's defiant words and spreads them before the Lord.

10. DO NOT LET YOUR GOD IN WHOM YOU TRUST DECEIVE YOU: Sennacherib had accused Hezekiah of deceiving the people concerning God's intentions and abilities, but here he went to the heart of his accusation by accusing God of being a deceiver. This blasphemy was at least as wicked as the previous one, as it essentially accused God of being the devil, who is the father of lies.

14. SPREAD IT BEFORE THE LORD: Hezekiah's act is a perfect picture of how God's people should deal with overwhelming threats, as he laid his difficulty out before the Lord. He was effectively saying, "Here is the letter I received, Lord. Please save us from this situation."

15. YOU HAVE MADE HEAVEN AND EARTH: Hezekiah expressed a fundamental truth: the One who created the earth is also God of the earth. The world of Hezekiah's day tried to deny this truth, just as it tries today, but it is an inescapable fact. There is only one God of the entire universe, and He rules it because He alone created it.

16. THE LIVING GOD: Hezekiah also touched on another fundamental truth: the Lord is the only living God, and all the other gods men serve are mere fictions. Only the Lord sees and hears and speaks, for the gods of the pagan world were man-made objects of wood and stone.

17. THE KINGS OF ASSYRIA HAVE LAID WASTE: Hezekiah did not gloss over the truth of his situation in his urgent prayer of supplication, nor did he attempt any false piety. He told the Lord frankly that the enemy spoke the truth

in their claims of crushing other nations and destroying their false gods. Yet in the process he did not lose sight of the truth of God's character, and he did not give in to fear, as the Assyrians hoped. He reminded himself that the enemy triumphed over other nations because their gods were not gods at all, while the Creator of the universe protected Judah.

19. THAT ALL THE KINGDOMS OF THE EARTH MAY KNOW: Hezekiah understood the Lord's larger purposes in His dealings with the nations. He protected the children of Israel because He had promised to do so, but His overall intention was that the world around Israel and Judah would come to a saving knowledge of Himself by seeing His faithfulness to them. The Lord is pleased when His people take His glory seriously.

> GOD'S RESPONSE: *The Lord hears Hezekiah's prayer and intervenes on behalf of His people. His glory will be shown throughout the earth.*

20. BECAUSE YOU HAVE PRAYED TO ME: The Lord's response to Hezekiah's prayer came through the prophet Isaiah. This statement from God is important, as it implies the Lord would deliver Judah from the Assyrians because they turned to Him for help. Israel, by contrast, had refused to humble themselves before the Lord, and so they had been taken into captivity.

22. WHOM HAVE YOU REPROACHED AND BLASPHEMED: The Lord took the Assyrians' words personally, even though much of their mockery was directed against Judah. The Lord identifies Himself with His people. What is done to His children is done to Him.

25. I HAVE BROUGHT IT TO PASS: Sennacherib thought he had accomplished his military victories through his own power and majesty, but the Lord laughed him to scorn. Those victories occurred because they were part of God's plan, and the Lord had used the Assyrians as a man might use a weapon. Sennacherib could not boast of conquering cities any more than a sword can boast of slaying foes. It is the One who wields the weapon who gets the glory.

34. I WILL DEFEND THIS CITY, TO SAVE IT: God's faithfulness was at stake in this contest with the Assyrians, for Sennacherib had directly challenged His faithfulness to His Word. The Lord did miraculously rescue the people, forcing Sennacherib to return home.

UNLEASHING THE TEXT

1) If you had been standing on the walls of Judah, listening to the Assyrian's words, how would you have responded? Why did Hezekiah command the people to remain silent?

_____

_____

_____

_____

2) What were the basic threats and accusations leveled by the Assyrian messenger? What truth was in his words? What lies were in those words?

_____

_____

_____

_____

3) What was the Assyrian messenger's goal in shouting his challenges at the people of Judah? How does the world attempt to do the same to Christians today?

_____

_____

_____

_____

4) What aspects of God's character did Hezekiah focus on in his prayers? How might his prayers serve as a model for our prayers when faced with difficult circumstances?

_____

_____

_____

EXPLORING THE MEANING

Do not be drawn into debate with sin. King Sennacherib's spokesman stood outside the walls of Judah, lying and blaspheming for all to hear. He accused Hezekiah of tearing down the Lord's sacred altars, mocked the army of Judah, claimed Sennacherib was bringing God's judgment on His people, defied the Lord, and denied the power of Judah's God. All the while, the people of Judah were atop the city walls, listening to the taunts of the Assyrians, hearing them blaspheme the Lord, enduring the threats of starvation and captivity—and answering not a word.

King Hezekiah demonstrated wisdom when he commanded them to remain silent. He did not want anyone to enter into debate with the enemy, for such debate leads only to further debate and eventually despair or sin. Eve literally met the devil in the Garden of Eden, and he lured her into a debate concerning the meaning of God's command. She stood and talked with him, and the conversation concluded when she reached out and sinned against God. The same principle applied to the people of Judah. The Assyrian was speaking the lies of the devil, and God's people were wise to remain silent.

Jesus demonstrated the best approach when confronted with the enemy's lies when He was fasting in the wilderness. When the devil came and tempted Him, His answer was to quote Scripture and say, "Get behind Me, Satan!" (Luke 4:8). There was no debate or interaction concerning the "deeper meanings" of Scripture—Christ simply meditated on God's Word and commanded the devil to depart. This is the model for us to follow whenever we are confronted by the lies of the Evil One: meditate on God's Word and call on Him to drive the enemy away.

Christians must know how to rightly divide God's Word. The Assyrians besieged the people of Judah with a war of words, using twisted logic, false statements, and threats to cast them into fear. What made it worse was that much of what they said was plausible. They pointed to their past victories over cities that were stronger than Judah and laid out what their plans were for starving them into submission. The propaganda reached its most dangerous level, however, when the Assyrians reminded the people of the words spoken by their own prophet Isaiah.

This principle is closely related to the previous one, for the devil loves to misuse God's Word to lead Christians astray. He used that tactic on Eve when he misquoted the Lord's command (see Genesis 3:1), and he even tried to misapply Scripture with Jesus, quoting verses to support sin (see Luke 4:9–11). But the Lord knew how to handle the Scriptures correctly, and His response to the devil's misapplied quotation was to counter with a more pertinent passage.

Paul addressed these important topics when he told Timothy to guard his flock against the dangers of idle debate and train them instead to become deeply rooted in the Word of God. "Be diligent to present yourself approved to God," wrote Paul, "a worker who does not need to be ashamed, rightly dividing the word of truth. But shun profane and idle babblings, for they will increase to more ungodliness" (2 Timothy 2:14–16). We learn to rightly divide God's Word by studying it, memorizing it, and asking God for wisdom in applying it.

God hears prayer. Hezekiah was overwhelmed with the threat facing his people. Assyria was the most powerful nation on earth, and the cruelty of its army was renowned. The recent defeat and captivity of Judah's fellow Jews in Israel was undoubtedly fresh in Hezekiah's mind. He had witnessed the Lord permit His people to be defeated by the Assyrians because of their idolatry, and he knew Judah had committed the same grievous sins. Now that same enemy was literally at his gates, openly declaring their intentions of destroying the city.

Yet Hezekiah did not give in to the fear that gripped him. Instead, he went into the house of God and spread before Him the defiant letter from Sennacherib, pouring out his heavy heart and asking the Lord to intervene. This was just what the Lord wanted, and He was pleased that His servant came to Him with his troubles instead of attempting to resolve them on his own. What's more, Hezekiah had taken an unbearable burden, a weight that he was not strong enough to carry, and had given it to the Lord to carry. He probably felt as though he was walking on air when he rose up from prayer that day.

In order to lay our burdens before God, we must first humble ourselves to the point of recognizing we are not strong enough to carry them. The Lord wants to bear our burdens for us, but He also wants us to ask for His help. It is pride that hinders our asking. "Be clothed with humility," Peter wrote to the church, "for 'God resists the proud, but gives grace to the humble.' Therefore humble yourselves under the mighty hand of God, that He may exalt you in due time, casting all your care upon Him, for He cares for you" (1 Peter 5:5–7).

REFLECTING ON THE TEXT

5) Why did God allow Israel to be taken into captivity by Assyria? Why did He not allow the same fate at this time for the people of Judah?

_____

_____

_____

6) In what ways does the world today try to engage Christians in futile debates? What should a Christian's response be to such debates?

_____

_____

_____

7) What does it mean to rightly divide the word of truth? How is this done? Why is it important for Christians to be able to do this?

_____

_____

_____

8) What does it mean to spread your troubles before the Lord? How can you do that? What troubles do you need to spread at His feet this week?

_____

_____

_____

PERSONAL RESPONSE

9) How diligent are you at present in understanding and applying God's Word? What will you do this week to grow stronger in this area?

_____

_____

_____

10) Are you jealous to guard the Lord's glory, as revealed through your life to others? Are there areas in your life that might be causing others to doubt His Word?

_____

_____

_____

10

Josiah Renews God's Word

2 Kings 22:1–23:25

Drawing Near

What are some ways that people can get into trouble if they don't know the rules of the land? Is it fair to hold people accountable to those rules if they are unaware the rules exist?

_____

_____

_____

The Context

The Lord miraculously delivered the people of Judah from the Assyrian army, forcing King Sennacherib to return to his capital of Nineveh. God had answered Hezekiah's prayer, and He would later even answer his request to heal to him from illness and extend his life by fifteen years. Sadly, Hezekiah's son Manasseh rebuilt all the high places his father had torn down. He reinstituted worship of Baal in Judah, and his son Amon followed in his footsteps.

Yet once again the Lord raised up a godly king in the person of Amon's son Josiah, who came to the throne was he was just eight years old. Josiah walked faithfully in obedience to God's Word throughout his life, and he was zealous to obey God in all things. Like King Hezekiah before him, Josiah removed the high places and utterly destroyed all remnants of pagan worship throughout Judah. He also commissioned a new building project to repair the temple, and when he did, the priests uncovered a lost book of God's law.

It is possible that Manasseh had destroyed all the copies of this book that were not hidden, and this had been the official copy laid beside the ark of the covenant. It had likely been removed from its place under the reign of Ahaz, Manasseh, or Amon, which is why it was only discovered when the repair work began. When Josiah heard the words of this book, he tore his clothes in mourning, for he knew that the Lord's wrath had been aroused against the people of Judah for not obeying God's law.

The Lord saw Josiah's humility and promised His judgment would not fall during his lifetime. Yet Josiah would prove to be the last king to lead the nation back to the Lord before that judgment fell. His example can help us avoid Judah's rebellious pattern of disobedience.

KEYS TO THE TEXT

Read 2 Kings 22:1–23:25, noting the key words and phrases indicated below.

THE LOST BOOK: King Josiah commands the repair to the temple in Jerusalem, where an interesting discovery is made.

22:1. THIRTY-ONE YEARS: Josiah ruled from 640–609 BC. Jeremiah, Zephaniah, and possibly Habakkuk were prophets to Judah during his reign. He was completely devoted to God's course of conduct for his life and obeyed the Mosaic stipulations as he came to know them. In this he followed the example of David, who set the pattern for the rulers of God's people.

4. THE MONEY WHICH HAS BEEN BROUGHT INTO THE HOUSE OF THE LORD: The temple had been repaired and refurbished under Jehoash, but it had once again fallen into disrepair. The neglect of God's temple coincided with the syncretism of the people. The more they added pagan elements to their worship, the less they frequented the temple in Jerusalem.

THE DOORKEEPERS: Josiah used the same procedure as King Jehoash for collecting funds to repair the temple after its abuse in the days of Manasseh and Amon.

8. THE BOOK OF THE LAW: This was probably a scroll containing a portion of Deuteronomy. The fact that it was discovered indicates it had been long forgotten—a tragic implication of the unfaithfulness of God's people, who had been entrusted with keeping the Lord's written revelation. Misplacing the book was a terrible dereliction of duty on the part of the Jews.

10. SHAPHAN READ IT BEFORE THE KING: Some believe that Shaphan read Deuteronomy 28–30, in which are recorded a renewal of the national covenant and a listing of the terrible threats and curses against all who violate the law of God.

CONFRONTED BY SIN: When the Book of the Law is read to the king, he is immediately disconcerted by what he hears and tears his clothes in anguish.

11. HE TORE HIS CLOTHES: King Josiah was overcome with grief because he realized God's people had completely forsaken His Law, and perhaps because he was shocked at his own ignorance of the sacred writings. Judah had been inventing their own religious methods and practices for so long they no longer knew what was written in God's Word.

13. GREAT IS THE WRATH OF THE LORD: The Lord had repeatedly warned His people not to serve the gods of the pagans but to study and obey His Word. He had also commanded them to be diligent in teaching His Word to their children to ensure that His people would not forget His commands and go after false gods. If the people failed to keep His Word, He had promised to remove them from the land of Canaan (see Deuteronomy 6).

14. HULDAH THE PROPHETESS: This prophetess is otherwise unknown in the Old Testament. She was held in some regard for her prophetic gift, though it is not clear why she and not some other prophet like Jeremiah or Zephaniah was consulted. God rarely spoke to the nation through a woman, and there is no record of a woman having an ongoing prophetic ministry.

THE SECOND QUARTER: This district was called *second* because it comprised the city's first major expansion. It was probably located on the western hill of Jerusalem in an area enclosed by the city wall and built during Hezekiah's reign. It is possible he had done this expansion to accommodate Jewish refugees who had escaped from the Assyrian invasion of Israel.

16. I WILL BRING CALAMITY: God told Josiah, through Huldah, that He was surely going to bring His judgment on Jerusalem because of the people's idolatry.

18. CONCERNING THE WORDS WHICH YOU HAVE HEARD: Josiah had been overwhelmed to discover his lack of knowledge of the Law, and he realized how far away the people had drifted from following it. He asked some of his servants to go before the Lord and seek His wisdom on what they needed to do concerning the Book of the Law.

19. YOUR HEART WAS TENDER: A tender heart is the opposite of a hard heart. It is malleable, like soft clay, allowing the Lord to shape it and mold it until it is similar to His own. Josiah had not hardened his heart in stubbornness when he read the Book of the Law but had humbled himself and repented of his sins. This is exactly what the Lord wants His people to do when they are convicted of sin. As David wrote, "The sacrifices of God are a broken spirit, a broken and a contrite heart these, O God, You will not despise" (Psalm 51:17).

20. TO YOUR GRAVE IN PEACE: The Lord's personal word to Josiah was that he would not witness the horrors that were in store for Jerusalem. However, he did die in battle.

PUBLIC READING OF GOD'S WORD: *King Josiah reads the Book of the Law to the entire nation of Judah, and they make a covenant of obedience.*

23:1. GATHER ALL THE ELDERS: The Lord had commanded the kings of Israel (and Judah) to write their copy of the Law by hand and read from it every day (see Deuteronomy 17:18–20). He had also commanded the priests to read the entire Law to the nation at least once every seven years (see 31:10–13). It is possible King Josiah discovered these commands in the fragment he read. It was a great tragedy that the priests of Judah did not possess a complete copy of the Law. All they had was this fragment, so even this public reading was incomplete.

3. MADE A COVENANT: Josiah fulfilled God's intended role for the kings of Israel and Judah by leading His people into obedience. He led by example, for he obeyed the Lord's commands in his own life so his people could have a role model to follow. Following Josiah's example, all the people promised to keep the stipulations of the Mosaic covenant.

WITH ALL HIS HEART AND ALL HIS SOUL: That is, inside and out, with his entire being—body, spirit, and mind. This phrase also harkens back to a passage known as the Shema: "Hear, O Israel: The LORD our God, the LORD is one! You shall love the LORD your God with all your heart, with all your soul, and with all your strength" (Deuteronomy 6:4–5).

CLEANSING THE LAND: Josiah not only has the Book of the Law read to the people but also takes steps to actually cleanse the land of all idolatry.

4. ALL THE ARTICLES THAT WERE MADE FOR BAAL: After the reading of the Law, Josiah took a number of steps to cleanse the land of its abominable practices. Unlike most of the prior kings, he also removed the high places. And when he removed an abomination, he did more than simply put it to one side—he burned it to ashes or ground it to powder.

CARRIED THEIR ASHES TO BETHEL: Bethel was located about ten miles north of Jerusalem and was one of the two original places where Jeroboam I had established an apostate worship center (see 1 Kings 12:28–33). The city was located just north of the border of Judah in the former northern kingdom, which was then the Assyrian province of Samaria. With a decline in Assyrian power, Josiah was able to exert his religious influence in the north. He used the ashes of the burned articles of idolatry to desecrate Jeroboam I's religious center.

6. GRAVES OF THE COMMON PEOPLE: The Kidron Valley contained a burial ground for the common people, and Josiah scattered ashes from the object of idolatry on the graves of those who sacrificed to that idol (see 2 Chronicles 34:4). The common people had followed their leaders to apostasy and damnation—all symbolized by the act of scattering the ashes.

7. RITUAL BOOTHS: These were tents used by women who were devoted to Asherah, in which they made hangings and committed sexual sins.

8. GEBA TO BEERSHEBA: Geba was located seven miles northeast of Jerusalem at the far north of Judah, and Beersheba was located forty-five miles south of Jerusalem at the southern end of Judah. This phrase was an idiomatic way of saying "throughout Judah."

10. HE DEFILED TOPHETH: This identified the area in the Valley of Hinnom where child sacrifice occurred. *Topheth* means "a drum," perhaps because drums were beaten there to drown out the cries of the children being sacrificed.

CLEANSING THE LAND: Josiah goes on to "defile" all the places that had been used for worshiping foreign gods, which effectively makes them unsuitable for such use in the future.

11. DEDICATED TO THE SUN. The horses and the chariots of the sun were probably thought to symbolize the sun blazing a trail across the sky. They were thus a part of worshiping the sun.

12. ON THE ROOF: Altars were erected on the flat roofs of houses so people could worship the "host of heaven" by burning incense.

13. ASHTORETH THE ABOMINATION OF THE SIDONIANS: Solomon had built high places east of Jerusalem on the Mount of Olives to be used in the worship of foreign gods, including the fertility goddess Ashtoreth from Sidon, the Moabite god Chemosh, and the Ammonite god Molech. These altars had existed for more than 300 years. The placing of human bones defiled them and, thus, rendered these sites unclean and unsuitable as places of worship.

15. THE ALTAR THAT WAS AT BETHEL: Josiah reduced the altar that Jeroboam I had built at Bethel to dust and ashes.

16. HE SAW THE TOMBS: Josiah saw tombs nearby—perhaps where idolatrous priests had been buried—and had their bones removed and burned on the altar at Bethel to defile it. This action fulfilled a prophecy given approximately 300 years before (see 1 Kings 13:2).

19. CITIES OF SAMARIA: The desecration of the high place at Bethel was only the beginning of Josiah's desecration of all the high places in the Assyrian province of Samaria.

20. EXECUTED ALL THE PRIESTS: These non-Levitical priests, who led apostate worship in the former northern kingdom, were idolaters who seduced God's people into idolatry. They were put to death in accordance with the statutes of the Law (see Deuteronomy 13:6–18; 17:2–7).

NO KING LIKE HIM: Josiah stands out among the list of kings in that he turned to the Lord with all his heart, all his soul, and all his might.

21. KEEP THE PASSOVER: Judah's celebration of this Passover more closely conformed to the instructions given in the Mosaic Law than any other in the previous 400 years of Israel's history. Although Hezekiah had observed the

Passover (see 2 Chronicles 30), no observance had been in exact conformity to God's law since the time of the judges.

23. IN THE EIGHTEENTH YEAR: All these reforms of Josiah took place c. 622 BC.

25. NO KING LIKE HIM: Of all the kings in David's line—including David himself—no king more closely approximated the royal ideal of Deuteronomy 17:14–20 than Josiah. Yet even Josiah fell short of complete obedience, because he had multiple wives. Unfortunately, as we will see in the next study, not even this righteous king could stop the people from turning back to foreign gods and incurring the Lord's wrath.

UNLEASHING THE TEXT

1) What made the Book of the Law so valuable? What might have led to its being lost? How did its being misplaced likely affect the people?

_____

_____

_____

_____

2) Why did King Josiah react so strongly when he was read the Book of the Law? What responsibilities had he and the priests of the land been neglecting?

_____

_____

_____

_____

3) Why did the Lord hold His people accountable to the Law even though it had been lost? Why did He show them mercy during this time?

_____

_____

_____

4) What does it mean to keep God's commandments with all one's heart and soul?

_____

_____

_____

EXPLORING THE MEANING

God requires a love for His Word. The Lord had given the people of Israel a sacred trust when He revealed Himself to them through His Law. The Israelites were the only people on earth who possessed such a collection of writings—God's Word spoken directly to His servant Moses. The Lord's intention was that Israel would be an example to the nations around them and show forth the grace and mercy of God to the Gentiles. To that end, the Lord commanded Israel to preserve His Word, guard it jealously, and pass it on faithfully.

Instead, the people forsook God's Word and began imitating the polytheistic nations around them. The process began with adding elements from pagan religions into their worship of the Lord, but gradually those pagan elements took precedence over God's Word. By the time of Josiah, the people had disregarded His Word for so long that it had been all but forgotten—and some of their sacred writings were evidently lost. This would not have happened if the Lord's people had obeyed His commands to teach His Word to their children.

Christians today have the same responsibility to God's Word. The Bible contains God's written revelation about Himself and provides everything we need "for doctrine, for reproof, for correction, for instruction in righteousness, that the man of God may be complete, thoroughly equipped for every good work" (2 Timothy 3:16–17). But if we are to gain its blessings, we must maintain its regular use in our homes and churches. We must also be diligent to teach God's Word to the next generation, training younger men and women to read it, meditate on it, and apply it to their lives. The example of Israel in Josiah's day must stand as a warning to God's people: keep His Word central in all things so it will never again be lost.

Keep your heart tender toward God's Word. The Lord commended King Josiah because his heart was tender, which means he was easily affected by a sense of his guilt before the Lord. When a wound is tender, it is sensitive to the touch and the slightest brushing will cause pain. This is the sense of the tender heart as well: a person with a tender heart is quick to recognize sin in his life, and that recognition causes pain and remorse. It is the opposite of a hard heart, which is insensitive to one's guilt and unresponsive to the Spirit's attempts to bring change.

Another metaphor is found in a lump of clay. A potter likes to work with clay that is soft and moldable because only then can he fashion it into a vessel fit for a king. When clay becomes hard it cannot be properly shaped, so the potter is forced to beat and knead the clay until it accepts moisture and becomes malleable once more. The human heart is prone to drying out and becoming hard like that lump of clay, which forces the Lord to use hardship and discipline to soften it up and make it fit for His hands.

The condition of our hearts is up to us. We harden or soften our hearts according to how we respond to God's Word. If we ignore its teachings, we will have hard hearts that become unresponsive to the Holy Spirit. However, if we are faithful and obedient to God's Word, we will have hearts that are soft and malleable. The writer of Hebrews warns us, "Beware, brethren, lest there be in any of you an evil heart of unbelief in departing from the living God; but exhort one another daily, while it is called 'Today,' lest any of you be hardened through the deceitfulness of sin" (Hebrews 3:12–13).

Scripture calls people to repent and obey without delay. King Josiah had been living in obedience to the Lord's commands as far as he understood them. He had walked in the ways of King David and followed the path of righteousness: "he did not turn aside to the right hand or to the left" (2 Chronicles 34:2). But one day, unexpectedly, he was handed God's Word to read—and he discovered the nation of Judah had been walking in disobedience for generations. Yet his response was exactly what the Lord desired. He did not try to justify his people's sins by claiming they didn't have the written Law, but instead humbled himself before the Lord and acknowledged that both he and his nation had fallen far short of God's commands.

This principle goes hand in hand with the previous one, since it is the method by which believers keep their hearts soft. There are times for all believers when the Lord draws our attention to an area of sin in our lives through His Word and His Spirit. He does this because He wants His children to grow into the image and likeness of Christ, which involves an ongoing process of purification. The Word of God functions with the indwelling help of His Spirit to show us areas that need to be brought into conformance with His image, and our part is to comply with His Spirit's promptings. The Lord wants His children to be responsive in this process, just as King Josiah was, and quick to address the areas He brings to our attention.

King David set an excellent example of this process. He had committed grievous sins of adultery and murder, and he had tried to continue on with his life as though he had done nothing wrong. But the Lord confronted him through His prophet Nathan, and David immediately confessed his sin and repented before the Lord (see 2 Samuel 12). King Jehoash, in contrast, set the opposite example. When the Lord's prophet confronted him with his sin, he became angry and hardened his heart, and his refusal to repent led him into even more grievous sins. John reminded his readers, "If we confess our sins, He is faithful and just to forgive us our sins and to cleanse us from all unrighteousness. If we say that we have not sinned, we make Him a liar, and His word is not in us" (1 John 1:9–10).

Reflecting on the Text

5) In your own words, what does it mean to have a tender heart? How does one keep his or her heart tender? Why is it important to do so?

---

6) How does God's Word become "lost"? What leads to this tragedy? How is it avoided?

_____

_____

_____

_____

7) Why is immediate repentance important when we sin? What leads a person to being convicted of sin? How is repentance accomplished?

_____

_____

_____

_____

8) When has God's Word convicted you of an area of disobedience of which you had been previously unaware? How did you respond?

_____

_____

_____

_____

PERSONAL RESPONSE

9) What are you doing at present to keep God's Word from being lost or forgotten? What are you doing to train the next generation in God's Word?

_____

_____

_____

_____

10) Compared to a lump of clay, what is the current state of your heart? Soft and malleable? Hard as a rock? Somewhere in between? What will you do this week to make it softer?

_____

_____

_____

_____

11

THE FALL OF JUDAH

2 Kings 23:31–25:30

DRAWING NEAR

What are some emotions people feel when they experience the death of a dream? What enables people to move on after their hopes have been dashed?

_____

_____

_____

THE CONTEXT

The nation of Judah had experienced an incredible revival during the reign of Josiah. Pagan shrines and centers of worship that had existed for centuries had been torn down and desecrated in order to prevent them from being rebuilt. Josiah had been a godly king like no other before him, and yet we read, "Nevertheless the LORD did not turn from the fierceness of His great wrath, with which His anger was aroused against Judah" (1 Kings 23:26).

It might seem surprising that the Lord would not forgo His wrath and judgment on the people after the reign of such a godly man. However, after Josiah is killed in battle, we see the people's hearts had already become hardened toward God. When Josiah's son Jehoahaz assumed the throne, the people quickly reverted to paganism. This same pattern had occurred repeatedly throughout Judah's history: a godly king would arise and turn the people to the Lord, and then an ungodly man would follow and turn them back to paganism.

During Josiah's reign, power in the ancient Near East shifted from Assyria to Babylon. The Babylonians destroyed Nineveh, the capital of Assyria, in 612 BC, and the Assyrian Empire fell soon after in 609 BC. God would use this rising power and a king named Nebuchadnezzar to finally end His people's depravity and carry them away into exile. Yet even in the midst of the Israelites' darkest hour—when all hope seemed lost and there was no chance of their return to their homeland—we discover God's mercy and grace in remembering His promises.

For after seventy years of captivity, the Lord would move the heart of another foreign king, a man named Cyrus, to allow His people to once again return to Jerusalem.

KEYS TO THE TEXT

Read 2 Kings 23:31–25:30, noting the key words and phrases indicated below.

BEGINNING OF THE END: King Josiah makes a foolish choice to go to war against the Egyptians. His death leads to Egyptian rule over the kingdom of Judah.

31. JEHOAHAZ . . . REIGNED THREE MONTHS: For some unstated reason, King Josiah was determined to stop Pharaoh Necho II and his army from joining with the Assyrians to fight the Babylonians. The Egyptians killed him at Megiddo, "and all Judah and Jerusalem mourned" his death (2 Chronicles 25:24). Josiah's son Jehoahaz took the throne in 609 BC, became a prisoner of Necho II that same year, and ultimately died in Egypt.

33. RIBLAH IN THE LAND: Necho II put Jehoahaz in prison at his military headquarters located on the Orontes River in the north Lebanon Valley. He then imposed a heavy tax on the people of Judah in the amount of 750 pounds of silver and seven-and-a-half pounds of gold.

34. CHANGED HIS NAME TO JEHOIAKIM: Necho II placed Jehoahaz's older brother on the throne and changed his name from Eliakim, meaning "God has established," to Jehoiakim, "the LORD has established." The naming

of a person in the ancient Near East was regarded as sign of authority, so by naming him Jehoiakim, Necho II was demonstrating that he was the lord who controlled Judah. As a vassal of Egypt, Judah risked attack by Egypt's enemy Babylon.

35. HE TAXED THE LAND: Jehoiakim taxed his people severely to pay the tribute to Egypt, though he still had enough to build a magnificent palace for himself (see Jeremiah 22:13–14).

36. HE REIGNED ELEVEN YEARS: Jehoiakim's reign was longer than his brother Jehoahaz's at eleven years (609–597 BC), but both of Josiah's sons did evil in God's eyes.

A NEW POWER: *King Nebuchadnezzar of Babylon conquers the Egyptians and assumes control of all of Egypt's vassal states— including Judah.*

24:1 NEBUCHADNEZZAR KING OF BABYLON: Nebuchadnezzar II was the son of Nabopolassar, the king of Babylon from 626–605 BC. As crown prince, Nebuchadnezzar led his father's army against Necho II and the Egyptians at Carchemish on the Euphrates River. By defeating the Egyptians, Babylon became the strongest nation in the ancient Near East.

JEHOIAKIM BECAME HIS VASSAL: Due to this victory, all of Egypt's vassals, including Judah, became vassals of Babylon. Nebuchadnezzar followed up his victory at Carchemish by invading the land of Judah. In 605 BC, Nebuchadnezzar took some captives to Babylon, including Daniel and his friends (see Daniel 1:1–3). Toward the end of that year, Nebuchadnezzar became king of Babylon, three years after Jehoiakim had taken the throne in Judah.

REBELLED AGAINST HIM: Nebuchadnezzar returned to the west in 604 BC and took tribute from all of the kings in the region, including Jehoiakim of Judah. Jehoiakim submitted to Babylonian rule but then rebelled against Babylon, disregarding the advice of the prophet Jeremiah (see Jeremiah 27:9–11).

2. THE LORD SENT AGAINST HIM RAIDING BANDS: As punishment for Jehoiakim's disobedience to the Lord's Word through His prophet Jeremiah, the Lord sent Babylonian troops, along with the troops of other loyal nations, to inflict military defeats on Judah.

7. KING OF EGYPT: In 601 BC Nebuchadnezzar again marched west against Egypt, but this time he was turned back by strong Egyptian resistance.

However, even though the Egyptian king was able defend his own land, he was not able to be aggressive and recover his conquered lands or provide any help for his allies, including Judah.

8. JEHOIACHIN WAS EIGHTEEN YEARS OLD: This reading is preferred over the "eight" of 2 Chronicles 36:9, because of the full development of his wickedness (see the prophet Ezekiel's description of him in Ezekiel 19:5–9).

HE REIGNED IN JERUSALEM THREE MONTHS: Nebuchadnezzar regrouped and invaded Judah for the second time in the spring of 597 BC. Before he could enter Jerusalem, Jehoiakim died and his son Jehoiachin succeeded him. Jehoiachin ruled for just three months that same year.

10. CAME UP AGAINST JERUSALEM: Nebuchadnezzar's troops began the siege of Jerusalem. Later, Nebuchadnezzar himself went to Jerusalem, and it was to the king himself that Jehoiachin surrendered.

12. IN THE EIGHTH YEAR OF HIS REIGN: For the first time, the author of Kings dates an event in Israelite history by a non-Israelite king. This indicates that Judah's exile is imminent and the land will soon be in the hands of Gentiles.

CAPTIVITY: *The Babylonians conquer Jerusalem, plunder the city's treasures, and take the leaders and the strong into captivity.*

13. CARRIED OUT FROM THERE ALL THE TREASURES: Nebuchadnezzar plundered the treasures of the temple and the king's palace, just as the Lord had said he would (see 2 Kings 20:16–18).

14. HE CARRIED INTO CAPTIVITY ALL JERUSALEM: Nebuchadnezzar took an additional 10,000 Judeans as captives to Babylon, in particular the leaders of the nation. This included the leaders of the military and those whose skills would support the military. Included in this deportation was the prophet Ezekiel.

16. ALL THE VALIANT MEN: The Babylonian policy of captivity was different from that of the Assyrians, who took most of the people into exile and resettled the land of Israel with foreigners. The Babylonians took only the leaders and the strong, while leaving behind the weak and the poor. They elevated those who were left to leadership, and in this way they earned their loyalty. Those taken to Babylon were allowed to work and live in the mainstream of society. This kept the Jews together, making it possible for them to return.

17. CHANGED HIS NAME TO ZEDEKIAH: Nebuchadnezzar placed Mattaniah, a son of Josiah and an uncle of Jehoiachin, on the throne and changed

his name from Mattaniah, meaning "gift of the LORD," to Zedekiah, meaning "righteousness of the LORD." Like Necho II before him, the Babylonian king changed his name to indicate his authority over him.

18. HE REIGNED ELEVEN YEARS: Zedekiah ruled in Jerusalem, under Babylonian sovereignty, from 597–586 BC. In 588 BC, Apries (also called Hophra), the grandson of Necho II, became the pharaoh over Egypt. He appears to have influenced Zedekiah to revolt against Babylon.

THE END OF JUDAH: The Babylonian king retaliates against Judah's rebellion by again invading Jerusalem, but this time he orders the city to be burned and dismantled.

25:1. IN THE NINTH YEAR: Nebuchadnezzar responded to Zedekiah's rebellion by sending his whole army to lay siege against Jerusalem. The siege wall was comprised of either wood towers higher than the walls of the city or a dirt rampart encircling the city.

2. UNTIL THE ELEVENTH YEAR: Jerusalem withstood the siege until the eleventh year of Zedekiah's reign, July of 586 BC. Hezekiah's tunnel guaranteed the city an uninterrupted supply of fresh water (see 2 Kings 20:20), and an Egyptian foray into Judah gave the city a temporary reprieve from the siege (see Jeremiah 37:5).

3. THE FAMINE HAD BECOME SO SEVERE: After a siege of more than two years, the food supply in Jerusalem finally ran out.

4. THE CITY WALL WAS BROKEN. The two walls near the king's garden were probably located at the extreme southeast corner of the city, giving direct access to the Kidron Valley. This provided Zedekiah and his soldiers an opportunity to flee for their lives to the east.

5. PLAINS OF JERICHO: Zedekiah fled toward the Jordan rift valley. Babylonian pursuers caught him in the Jordan Valley south of Jericho, about twenty miles east of Jerusalem.

6. AT RIBLAH: This town, located on the Orontes River about 180 miles north of Jerusalem, was Nebuchadnezzar's military headquarters during his invasion of Judah. The location was ideally situated as a field headquarters for military forces because ample provisions could be found nearby.

7. PUT OUT THE EYES: The captured traitor Zedekiah was brought to Nebuchadnezzar and blinded after witnessing the death of his sons. The execution of the royal heirs ensured the impossibility that Zedekiah's descendants could

claim the throne or stage another rebellion. The prophet Jeremiah had warned Zedekiah that he would see Nebuchadnezzar (see Jeremiah 34:3), while Ezekiel had said he would not see Babylon (see Ezekiel 12:13). Both prophecies accurately came to pass.

8. SEVENTH DAY OF THE MONTH: Nebuzaradan, the commander of Nebuchadnezzar's imperial guard, arrived one month after the Babylonians broke through Jerusalem's walls to oversee the city's destruction (August 586 BC).

THE TEMPLE IS BURNED: The Babylonians set fire to the temple that King Solomon had built, signaling the end of God's presence in Jerusalem.

9. BURNED THE HOUSE OF THE LORD: The Babylonians carried out the dismantling and burning of the city in an orderly progression. They first burned down Jerusalem's most important buildings and then tore down Jerusalem's outer walls (the city's main defense). This burning of the temple marked the end for the nations of Judah and Israel, as it demonstrated God had removed His presence from His holy city of Jerusalem. He had not abandoned His people, but when His Spirit left the temple, it was an expression that the people had abandoned Him.

11. CARRIED AWAY CAPTIVE: Nebuzaradan organized and led a forced march of the remaining Judeans into exile in Babylon. The exiles included survivors from Jerusalem and those who had surrendered to the Babylonians before the capture of the city. As before, only the poor, unskilled laborers were left behind to tend the vineyards and farm the fields.

13. CARRIED THEIR BRONZE TO BABYLON: Nebuzaradan then carried away to Babylon the items made with precious metals in the temple.

20. BROUGHT THEM TO THE KING OF BABYLON: Finally, Nebuzaradan took Jerusalem's remaining leaders to Riblah, where Nebuchadnezzar had them executed. This insured they would never lead another rebellion against Babylon. Seraiah was the grandson of the priest of Hilkiah (see 2 Kings 22:3–8) and an ancestor of Ezra. Even though the Babylonians executed Seraiah, they deported his sons (see 1 Chronicles 6:15)

21. CAPTIVE FROM ITS OWN LAND: Exile was the ultimate curse brought on Judah because of the people's disobedience to the Mosaic covenant. In Lamentations, the prophet Jeremiah records the sorrow the people felt at the destruction of Jerusalem.

LIFE AFTER CONQUEST: The author of Kings concludes his book by showing that in spite of God's punishment, the people of Israel and Judah remained rebellious.

22. GEDALIAH THE SON OF AHIKAM: In an attempt to maintain political stability, Nebuchadnezzar appointed a governor from an important Judean family. Gedaliah's grandfather, Shaphan, was Josiah's secretary, who had implemented that king's reforms. His father, Ahikam, was part of Josiah's delegation sent to Huldah and a supporter of the prophet Jeremiah.

23. AT MIZPAH: This city, located about eight miles north of Jerusalem, became the new center of Judah. Mizpah might have been one of the few towns left standing after the Babylonian invasion.

24. TOOK AN OATH: As governor, Gedaliah pledged to the remaining people that loyalty to the Babylonians would ensure their safety.

25. IT HAPPENED IN THE SEVENTH MONTH: In October 586 BC, just two months after the destruction of Jerusalem, a man named Ishmael assassinated Gedaliah. It is likely that Ishmael wished to reestablish the kingship in Judah with himself as king, as he was of royal blood.

26. WENT TO EGYPT: Fearing reprisals from the Babylonians, the people fled to Egypt.

27. EVIL-MERODACH: This son and successor of Nebuchadnezzar ruled as king of Babylon from 562–560 BC. To gain favor with the Jews, the king released Jehoiachin from his imprisonment and gave him special privileges. Jehoiachin was fifty-five years old at the time.

28. SPOKE KINDLY TO HIM: This good word from the king of Babylon to the surviving representative of the house of David served as a concluding reminder of God's good word to David. Through the curse of exile, the dynasty of David had survived. There was still hope that God's good word to David about the seed who would build God's temple and establish God's eternal kingdom would be fulfilled (see 2 Samuel 7:12–16).

30. ALL THE DAYS OF HIS LIFE: The book of 2 Kings opened with Elijah being carried away to heaven, the destination of all those faithful to God. The book ends with Israel, and then Judah, being carried away to pagan lands as a result of failing to be faithful to God. But the author of Chronicles provides a ray of hope: after seventy years of captivity, the Lord would move Cyrus of Persia to release some of His people to return to Jerusalem (see 2 Chronicles 36:23).

Unleashing the Text

1) What outside forces brought about the fall of Jerusalem and Judah? What does this tell you about God's hand in world events—even those that seem dark and foreboding?

_____

_____

_____

2) How were the kings and rulers of Judah chosen during the time following Josiah's death? How did this impact the nation of Judah?

_____

_____

3) What tactics did the Babylonians use to subdue the people of Judah? How did the leaders of Judah respond? What were the results?

_____

_____

_____

4) Based on 2 Kings 23:26–27, what was God's involvement in the fall of Judah? What events show that God had withdrawn His presence from His people?

_____

_____

_____

EXPLORING THE MEANING

Seek the Lord, and He will be found. Throughout these studies, we have encountered the theme of seeking God. Some of the kings of Judah sought God, many did not, but in both cases the seeker always found what he was seeking. King Josiah sought the Lord, and he found him. But his son Jehoahaz put his trust in idols, and he found them. The end result of each choice is self-evident: seeking the Lord leads to life, while seeking idols leads to death. One wonders why anyone would ever choose to *not* seek God.

Yet many Christians likewise try to coast through life taking the easy route. They believe that by not actively seeking false gods, they are actively seeking God. But that is not the case, for seeking God is more than not seeking idols. It is an active pursuit—something that believers must deliberately choose to do. This is done by studying God's Word on a regular basis; by meeting with other believers regularly for worship, Bible study, and prayer; and by regular times of prayer and confession privately before the Lord. It also requires that we be on guard at all times to ensure that nothing else in life ever takes a higher priority than the pursuit of God. If we choose to not make this deliberate choice, we are effectively choosing to not seek God.

The good news is that the process of seeking God is not burdensome or difficult. Indeed, the Lord is busier seeking us than we could ever be seeking Him, and He so wants us to find Him that He was willing to sacrifice His Son on the cross to make it possible. All that is required of us is to humble ourselves before Him, confess our sins, and submit to His lordship in all areas of our lives. When we do this, He has promised that He will be found. "Draw near to God and He will draw near to you. Cleanse your hands, you sinners; and purify your hearts, you double-minded. . . . Humble yourselves in the sight of the Lord, and He will lift you up" (James 4:8, 10).

Love God wholeheartedly. Again and again in these studies, we have encountered the admonition to love God with all our hearts. What exactly does this mean? To love God with all our hearts means that we are to love God with every aspect of our being, including our thoughts and affections. The heart is the part of us that thinks and wills and makes determinations. It is the seat of our conscious volition.

In a theological sense, our obedience to God begins with God Himself, for it is only through His power and intervention in our lives that we are able to obey Him in any respect. However, from a human perspective, our obedience and commitment to God's Word begins with our hearts, our minds, and our volition—and particularly with our thoughts. This is the reason we are commanded to guard our hearts, as Solomon warned when he wrote, "Keep your heart with all diligence, for out of it spring the issues of life" (Proverbs 4:23). We become wholehearted for God by first deciding in our hearts and minds that it is our top priority.

Our thinking determines who we become. The story of Israel and Judah is that the natural man or woman wants to think about fleshly pursuits, but this only leads a person to become conformed to the image of the world. Christians are called to change from fleshly thinking to godly thinking—and this is the first step in becoming wholehearted for God. Paul wrote, "I beseech you therefore, brethren, by the mercies of God, that you present your bodies a living sacrifice, holy, acceptable to God, which is your reasonable service. And do not be conformed to this world, but be transformed by the renewing of your mind, that you may prove what is that good and acceptable and perfect will of God" (Romans 12:1–2).

God does not forget His people. The Israelites were going through a terrifying time in their history. Their daily lives were characterized by political unrest, famine, siege, starvation, exile, and abrupt changes in leadership. Many of those who had remained faithful to the Lord must have wondered if He still remembered them. When Judah fell, they must have also wondered how God would fulfill His promise to David that his kingdom would endure forever (see 2 Samuel 7:12–16). For them, it must have seemed as if all their hopes had come to an end.

What the Israelites could not have known was that God was working behind the scenes to keep them intact as a people group. The time of their exile would be long, but the Lord would raise up leaders to protect them and guide them in their captivity. "This whole land shall be a desolation and an astonishment," the Lord promised them, "and these nations shall serve the king of Babylon seventy years. Then it will come to pass, when seventy years are completed, that I will punish the king of Babylon and that nation" (Jeremiah 25:11–12).

In the end, the Lord would reveal He had never forgotten His people by moving the heart of a Persian king named Cyrus to allow them to return home. Centuries later, many of the Jews would also discover that God had not forgotten His promise to David—for through his line came Jesus Christ, the promised eternal King. Today, believers in Christ have that same assurance that God will always be with them, for Jesus promised, "If I go and prepare a place for you, I will come again and receive you to Myself; that where I am, there you may be also" (John 14:3).

REFLECTING ON THE TEXT

5) How did God set the stage for the fulfillment of His promise to David through the destruction of Jerusalem and the people's exile to Babylon?

_____

_____

_____

6) In what ways were the people of Judah vulnerable to sin? What did they fail to do that promoted the tolerance of and indulgence in pagan worship?

_____

_____

_____

7) In what ways is our culture passive toward sin? Why do you think our culture tolerates sin? What roles do we as believers have in turning our culture toward faith in God?

_____

_____

_____

_____

8) What challenges seem to stand in the way of God triumphing over evil in our world? What is our source of hope in the face of circumstances that seem overwhelming?

_____

_____

_____

PERSONAL RESPONSE

9) What is your first response to the presence of evil in your world? What motivates your response? What role can God's Word play in reinforcing your faith in the Lord's sovereignty when circumstances make this difficult?

_____

_____

_____

10) Who in your life needs to know that God is actively seeking to establish or restore a love-relationship with him or her? What words of hope or encouragement can you share with that person? What picture of God can you show him or her?

_____

_____

_____

12

REVIEWING KEY PRINCIPLES

DRAWING NEAR

As you look back at each of the studies in 2 Kings, what is the one thing that stood out to you the most? What is one new perspective you have learned?

_____

_____

_____

THE CONTEXT

During the last eleven studies, you have examined some of the prophets and priests that God raised up to guide His people and lead them back to His ways. You have seen how the kings of Israel for the most part ignored these men of God and continued to lead their people into idolatry. You have also witnessed a repetitive cycle in Judah of godly kings instituting great revivals followed by ungodly kings who lead the people back into pagan worship.

Ultimately, you have seen how God's judgment finally fell on Israel in the form of the Assyrian army and on Judah in the form of the Babylonian captivity. Yet even in this you have seen that the Lord was faithful to His people and His promises, for after seventy years in exile He would begin to bring His people back to Jerusalem. This truth echoes the theme that has remained constant throughout these studies: _God is faithful, and those who obey Him will grow in faithfulness as well._

Here are a few of the major principles we have found during our study. There are many more we don't have room to reiterate, so take some time to review the earlier studies—or, better still, to meditate on the Scripture that we have covered. As you do, ask the Holy Spirit to give you wisdom and insight into His Word. He will not refuse.

EXPLORING THE MEANING

The battle belongs to God, but we also have a role to play. Jehoshaphat recognized that his people were powerless to defeat the terrible foe that came to destroy them, and he turned to the Lord for deliverance. This was exactly the right response, for the Lord wants His people to let Him fight their battles. God promised the king that He would rout the foe, "for the battle is not yours, but God's" (2 Chronicles 20:15).

Nevertheless, this promise did not give the people of Judah the right to go home and take a nap until the war was over. The Lord was indeed going to do the fighting for them, but they still had a part to play in the conflict. It was not an aggressive part—on the contrary, their role was to take a position, stand firm in it, and watch. Their task was to trust the Lord would keep His promises and then stand firm in that faith even though they were faced with an enemy that threatened to destroy them. By standing firm in their faith, they were free to watch for God's great deliverance—and when it came, they saw their faith was not in vain.

This is what it means to stand strong in the faith. We have the steadfast assurance that God will always keep His promises, and we can fully depend on Him to protect us and fight on our behalf against the enemy who seeks to destroy us. When we are firm in our faith, we can see God at work in our lives for His glory, and we can also realize that all the glory belongs to God. He will deliver us, and we will surely see that our faith is not in vain.

God makes us His heirs through Christ. Elisha's request to inherit a double portion of Elijah's spirit is significant. His request was the equivalent of asking to be made Elisha's spiritual heir, his firstborn, responsible for carrying on the ministry that God had given to Elijah. In biblical times, the firstborn son was always the successor of the head of a family, and he received all the status and power that accompanied that position. Note that Elisha didn't make this request out of a desire for power, but because he knew the work ahead would require it. The Bible records twice as many miracles performed through Elisha than through Elijah.

Believers in Christ, having received the adoption of the Spirit, are given this same status as heirs. As Paul wrote, "For as many as are led by the Spirit of God, these are sons of God. For you did not receive the spirit of bondage again to fear, but you received the Spirit of adoption by whom we cry out, "Abba, Father" (Romans 8:14–15). Furthermore, Jesus promises that when we take on His mantle, we will do even greater works than He performed (see John 14:12).

Like the prophet Elisha, we face a world today in which people have turned their hearts from God. Just like Elisha, we need a "double portion" of God's power to fulfill the great commission He has given to us to share the good news of Christ with a lost and hurting world. God provides this power in abundance to us through the gift of the Holy Spirit dwelling within us. As Jesus said to His followers, "You shall receive power when the Holy Spirit has come upon you; and you shall be witnesses" (Acts 1:8).

God is in control of life and death. Elisha faced the timeless dilemma: what to get the woman who had everything. Unlike the widow who was on the verge of starvation, the Shunammite woman had wealth and a husband. However, she was also barren, and it seems that she had given up hope of ever having a child. Elisha knew that only God could give life, and thus if she received a baby it would be obvious that it was a gift from the Lord.

But when the child later died, the Shunammite woman knew that this, too, was from the Lord. She did not blame her husband, sickness, or any other factor for the boy's death but instead went straight to the man of God. Likewise, Elisha knew the child's death was from the Lord. In fact, it was obvious that no power inherent in Elisha raised the boy to life; rather, it was God who answered Elisha's fervent prayer. Just as the boy's death was from the Lord, so too was his new life.

Many centuries earlier, a man named Job had lost his children to untimely deaths. When his family was killed by demonically inspired but divinely permitted marauders, Job declared, "The LORD gave, and the LORD has taken away" (Job 1:21). Later he asked his wife, "Shall we indeed accept good from God, and shall we not also accept adversity?" (Job 2:10). Job understood that all life is under the control of God. For this reason, we can have confidence in the face of death, but we can also rejoice that our God is the author of life.

The sin of covetousness can destroy a person's ministry. Gehazi was privileged to work beside Elisha and had a unique ministry. He assisted the prophet in performing great miracles, and he was blessed with hearing the Word of God, day in and day out, right from the mouth of God's chief spokesman in Israel. He probably also had a great ministry ahead of him, as Elisha was evidently training him to take on the mantle of prophetic leadership when the time came. These things indicate he was a godly man who was qualified for such a ministry as few others would have been. He undoubtedly had some rough edges, as we all do, but the Lord was at work to smooth out those rough spots and equip him for greater areas of service.

But Gehazi was dazzled by the immense wealth of Naaman's gift—enough gold and silver for him to live in comfort for the rest of his days. He also coveted honor and prestige, as he walked behind two servants who carried his newfound loot like a triumphant warrior returning from battle. Perhaps Gehazi justified such indulgences by telling himself how he would use the wealth and honor to further the Lord's work. But even such excuses do not justify greed. The truth is that he had "cashed in" on God's grace, using God's work of salvation for his own material gain—and this sin resulted in permanent damage to his ministry.

Gehazi's sin did not end his walk with God, for he appeared later still serving Elisha. However, it did damage his testimony and severely hinder his future effectiveness in ministry. This principle holds true for any area of sin. The Lord does not abandon His children when they indulge in sinful behavior, but such disobedience may permanently disqualify us from future areas of service. The Bible instructs us on how to avoid the tragedy of Gehazi: "Do not love the world or the things in the world. If anyone loves the world, the love of the Father is not in him. For all that is in the world—the lust of the flesh, the lust of the eyes, and the pride of life—is not of the Father but is of the world" (1 John 2:15–16).

Avoid the sin of ingratitude. King Jehoash owed a great deal to the spiritual leadership of Jehoiada—indeed, he owed very his life to the high priest and his wife. Yet Jehoiada's gifts did not end with the preservation of Jehoash's life, for the high priest undoubtedly taught the young boy from the Word of God during the years he was living at the temple. Jehoiada later gathered the people together and made Jehoash king, again at great risk to himself, and continued to counsel him in the ways of righteousness.

But Jehoash "did not remember the kindness which Jehoiada his father had done to him" (2 Chronicles 24:22), and this same forgetfulness led him into a great sin. How could a man forget such costly and selfless love, especially when he owed his kingship and his life to the man who had been like a father to him? The answer is found in the heart of every human being. Jehoash fell into ingratitude because he forgot to remember the goodness God had shown to him. We also fall into ingratitude when we fail to remember the goodness of God.

Gratitude requires effort on our part to remember the blessings we have received through the efforts of others. This is the reason the Bible commands us to deliberately remember all the Lord has done on our behalf, for without such deliberate recollection, we will quickly take His love and kindness for granted. As King David wrote, "Bless the LORD, O my soul, and forget not all His benefits" (Psalm 103:2). This is done by choosing to rejoice rather than complain, by intentionally focusing on a spirit of thankfulness, and by taking our gratitude directly to God. Paul wrote, "Rejoice always, pray without ceasing, in everything give thanks; for this is the will of God in Christ Jesus for you" (1 Thessalonians 5:16–18).

Occult activities are an attempt to replace God. The idolatry of Israel began as syncretism, but it ended with the most hideous abominations, including child sacrifice. This was a clear testimony that the Israelites thought the one true God was insufficient to guide them and they needed protection and direction from other gods. While child sacrifice may sound like an extreme case, the fact is that all disobedience to God's Word eventually leads to abominable practices if we do not repent and turn away from disobedience.

By definition, sin is the act of choosing to follow inner desires rather than submitting to God, and all sin leads inexorably away from the Lord and toward evil. Interestingly, the Lord includes child sacrifice in the category of occult abominations. Today this is practiced through the widespread sin of abortion. It is no coincidence that as Western civilization hardens its heart against God, sins like these are becoming more accepted.

Christians, of course, must have no part in this. God strictly forbade His people to even associate with "anyone who makes his son or his daughter pass through the fire, or one who practices witchcraft, or a soothsayer, or one who interprets omens, or a sorcerer, or one who conjures spells, or a medium, or a spiritist, or one who calls up the dead. For all who do these things are an abomination to the LORD, and because of these abominations the LORD your God drives them out from before you" (Deuteronomy 18:10–12). As Christians, our direction and protection is found in the Lord, not through other means such as the sacrifice of children.

God hears prayer. Hezekiah was overwhelmed with the threat facing his people. Assyria was the most powerful nation on earth, and the cruelty of its army was renowned. The recent defeat and captivity of Judah's fellow Jews in Israel was undoubtedly fresh in Hezekiah's mind. He had witnessed the Lord permit His people to be defeated by the Assyrians because of their idolatry, and he knew Judah had committed the same grievous sins. Now that same enemy was literally at his gates, openly declaring their intentions of destroying the city.

Yet Hezekiah did not give in to the fear that gripped him. Instead, he went into the house of God and spread before Him the defiant letter from Sennacherib, pouring out his heavy heart and asking the Lord to intervene. This was just what the Lord wanted, and He was pleased that His servant came to Him with his troubles instead of attempting to resolve them on his own. What's more, Hezekiah had taken an unbearable burden, a weight that he was not strong enough to carry, and had given it to the Lord to carry. He probably felt as though he was walking on air when he rose up from prayer that day.

In order to lay our burdens before God, we must first humble ourselves to the point of recognizing we are not strong enough to carry them. The Lord wants to bear our burdens for us, but He also wants us to ask for His help. It is pride that hinders our asking. "Be clothed with humility," Peter wrote to the church, "for 'God resists the proud, but gives grace to the humble.' Therefore humble yourselves under the mighty hand of God, that He may exalt you in due time, casting all your care upon Him, for He cares for you" (1 Peter 5:5–7).

Keep your heart tender toward God's Word. The Lord commended King Josiah because his heart was tender, which means he was easily affected by a sense of his guilt before the Lord. When a wound is tender, it is sensitive to the touch and the slightest brushing will cause pain. This is the sense of the tender heart as well: a person with a tender heart is quick to recognize sin in his life, and that recognition causes pain and remorse. It is the opposite of a hard heart, which is insensitive to one's guilt and unresponsive to the Spirit's attempts to bring change.

Another metaphor is found in a lump of clay. A potter likes to work with clay that is soft and moldable because only then can he fashion it into a vessel fit for a king. When clay becomes hard it cannot be properly shaped, so the potter is forced to beat and knead the clay until it accepts moisture and becomes malleable once more. The human heart is prone to drying out and becoming hard like that lump of clay, which forces the Lord to use hardship and discipline to soften it up and make it fit for His hands.

The condition of our hearts is up to us. We harden or soften our hearts according to how we respond to God's Word. If we ignore its teachings, we will have hard hearts that become unresponsive to the Holy Spirit. However, if we are faithful and obedient to God's Word, we will have hearts that are soft and malleable. The writer of Hebrews warns us, "Beware, brethren, lest there be in any of you an evil heart of unbelief in departing from the living God; but exhort one another daily, while it is called 'Today,' lest any of you be hardened through the deceitfulness of sin" (Hebrews 3:12–13).

UNLEASHING THE TEXT

1) Which of the concepts or principles in this study have you found to be the most encouraging? Why?

_____

_____

_____

_____

_____

2) Which of the concepts or principles have you found most challenging? Why?

_____

_____

_____

_____

3) What aspects of "walking with God" are you already doing in your life? Which areas need strengthening?

_____

_____

_____

_____

_____

4) To which of the characters that we've studied have you most been able to relate? How might you emulate that person in your own life?

_____

_____

_____

_____

_____

PERSONAL RESPONSE

5) Have you taken a definite stand for Jesus Christ? Have you accepted His free gift of salvation? If not, what is preventing you from doing so?

_____

_____

_____

_____

6) What areas of your life have been most convicted during this study? What exact things will you do to address these convictions? Be specific.

_____

_____

_____

_____

7) What have you learned about the character of God during this study? How has this insight affected your worship or prayer life?

_____

_____

_____

_____

_____

8) What are some specific things you want to see God do in your life in the coming month? What are some things you intend to change in your own life during that time? (Return to this list in one month and hold yourself accountable to fulfill these things.)

_____

_____

_____

_____

If you would like to continue in your study of the Old Testament, read the next title in this series: *Daniel and Esther: Israel in Exile.*

ALSO AVAILABLE

In this study, John MacArthur guides readers through an in-depth look at the historical period beginning with God's calling of Moses, continuing through the giving of the Ten Commandments, and concluding with the Israelites' preparations to enter the Promised Land. This study includes close-up examinations of Aaron, Caleb, Joshua, Balaam and Balak, as well as careful considerations of doctrinal themes such as "Complaints and Rebellion" and "Following God's Law."

The MacArthur Bible Studies provide intriguing examinations of the whole of Scripture. Each guide incorporates extensive commentary, detailed observations on overriding themes, and probing questions to help you study the Word of God with guidance from John MacArthur.

ALSO AVAILABLE

JOHN MACARTHUR

JOSHUA,
JUDGES & RUTH

FINALLY IN THE LAND

MacArthur Bible Studies

In this study, John MacArthur guides readers through an in-depth look at the Israelites' conquest of the Promised Land, beginning with the miraculous parting of the Jordan River, continuing through the victories and setbacks as the people settled into Canaan, and concluding with the time of the judges. Studies include close-up examinations of Rahab, Ruth, and Samson, as well as careful considerations of doctrinal themes such as "The Sin of Achan" and the role of "The Kinsman Redeemer."

The MacArthur Bible Studies provide intriguing examinations of the whole of Scripture. Each guide incorporates extensive commentary, detailed observations on overriding themes, and probing questions to help you study the Word of God with guidance from John MacArthur.

ALSO AVAILABLE

In this study, John MacArthur guides readers through an in-depth look at this historical period beginning with the miraculous birth of Samuel, continuing through Saul's crowning as Israel's first king, and concluding with his tragic death. Studies include close-up examinations of Hannah, Eli, Saul, David, and Jonathan, as well as careful considerations of doctrinal themes such as "Slaying a Giant" and "Respecting God's Anointed."

The MacArthur Bible Studies provide intriguing examinations of the whole of Scripture. Each guide incorporates extensive commentary, detailed observations on overriding themes, and probing questions to help you study the Word of God with guidance from John MacArthur.

ALSO AVAILABLE

JOHN MACARTHUR

2 SAMUEL

DAVID'S HEART REVEALED

MacArthur Bible Studies

In this study, John MacArthur guides readers through an in-depth look at the historical period beginning with David's struggle to establish his throne, continuing through his sin and repentance, and concluding with the tragic rebellion of his son Absalom. Studies include close-up examinations of Joab, Amnon, Tamar, Absalom, and others, as well as careful considerations of doctrinal themes such as "Obedience and Blessing" and being a "Man After God's Own Heart."

The MacArthur Bible Studies provide intriguing examinations of the whole of Scripture. Each guide incorporates extensive commentary, detailed observations on overriding themes, and probing questions to help you study the Word of God with guidance from John MacArthur.

9780718034740-A